The Solution Path

Your Guide to
Turning Workplace Problems
into Opportunities

Tasos Sioukas

First published in 2003 by Jossey Bass Publishers, a Wiley Imprint

New edition 2011 by Anastasios Sioukas

Library of Congress Pre-assigned Control Number is on file at the Library of Congress, Washington, DC.

ISBN 978-0983-7551-59

Praise for *The Solution Path*

"After leading problem-solving sessions for decades, I was confident in my approach. *The Solution Path* has challenged me to reexamine my work by posing challenging questions and offering new tools. This book provides important insights for everyone engaged in any improvement effort."
— Ingrid Bens, author, *Facilitating With Ease*

"This is a brilliant book. Once I started to read it, I couldn't put it down. *The Solution Path* will help readers to discover and capitalize on their strengths as well as assist managers to optimize their day to day activities with their teams."
— Robert Thunholm, Shriners Hospital for Children, Los Angeles

"*The Solution Path* will help you demystify the processes of effectively working with teams, of envisioning outcomes and developing ideas, and finally, it will empower you to formulate and deliver a strategically sound solution to your problem. It does so by using solid, graspable concepts, and creative, hands-on tools. This book delivers!"
— Marios Stilianakis, *Odyssey Magazine*

"Any manager who wants to lead employees toward innovation and solutions will find that Tasos has brought together all the best practices of group work in a refreshing, easy-to-understand package. He integrates the elements of success with a deep appreciation for the spiritual side of this kind of work."
— Kathleen S. Whiteside, partner, Performance International

Reviews for *The Solution Path*

"The back cover states that "Sioukas presents practical solution-finding methods, with an emphasis on positive thinking, relationships, teamwork, and creativity. Sioukas shows you how to put fear aside… and create opportunities." It's true."
— *The Facilitator*

"Positive thinking, teamwork, relationship-building and creativity are all ideals of the workplace; but just how do problems become turned around so these ideals can be fostered and encouraged to develop? Turn to Tasos Sioukas' *The Solution Path*… for insights into just how."
— *Midwest Book Review*

"The Solution Path maximizes the collective genius of teams while achieving buy-in and commitment for lasting organizational change."
— Society for Human Resource Management

"The Solution Path shows you how to turn workplace problems into opportunities."
— *New Equipment Digest*

"The results of this methodology are amazing."
— *Arizona Networking News*

"Sioukas extends boundaries by addressing aspects of problem solving not usually considered."
— *Quality Progress*

"An excellent guide."
— Stern and Associates

Contents

To my parents . . .

Acknowledgements

I would like to thank my clients and the thousands of executives, managers, administrators, professionals, and students who attend my seminars and classes. My clients give me the opportunity to partner with them in their efforts for change and innovation and challenge me with difficult questions. The individuals who take my seminars and classes that integrate *The Solution Path* continuously provide new suggestions and ideas. Together we all share the lessons that shape the methods and tools of *The Solution Path*.

This book was originally published by Jossey-Bass. I am very grateful to Susan Williams for her encouragement and support. I also owe thanks to Byron Schneider and Tamara Keller from the editorial team, and numerous other individuals for their help.

Several friends and colleagues read the book and I thank them for their constructive input and encouragement. In addition, I owe thanks to the individuals who read and endorsed *The Solution Path*, and particularly Ingrid Bens, Richard Chang, Johan Roos, and Kathleen Whiteside. I am especially thankful to Ingrid Bens and Marios Stilianakis for their valuable input to this edition.

A special thanks to Lyn Adelstein who worked on the cover and the typesetting of this new edition, and made the process simple and fun. I am also indebted to my family members for their encouragement and support

Finally, I am eternally grateful to my Higher Power for enabling me to develop this work. In turn, I offer *The Solution Path* to all of you with the wish that it will inspire you to look beyond challenges, stretch your imagination and visualize ideal outcomes, develop ideas, build solutions, and embark on journeys to new opportunities.

The Author

Tasos Sioukas is an internationally recognized consultant, trainer, and educator. He is the director of The Sigma Organization, a firm founded to facilitate growth and innovation. He has partnered with executive teams at hundreds of clients to support them in discovering and implementing creative change solutions.

Sioukas focuses on enabling clients to build and mobilize their own capacity for individual and collective creativity. Thousands of executives, administrators, consultants, engineers, scientists, and community leaders have benefited from his skill-building seminars.

An effective multicultural facilitator, Sioukas has worked and lived in the United States and Europe and speaks four languages, English, Greek, Spanish, and French. He is a professor of Business and Management at Los Angeles Valley College and also teaches at the University of Southern California (USC). He has published numerous articles in both the popular and academic press and has won international awards from such institutions as the Academy of Management, the National Academy of Engineering, and the Economic Development Network of California.

Sioukas earned his doctorate degree from USC in a self-conceived program in the management of change and innovation and holds a master's degree in industrial engineering from the University of California at Berkeley. He currently lives in Los Angeles.

For further information, please see www.the-sigma.com.

Introduction

Problem solving is one of the most valuable and sought-after skills. It is ranked consistently among the top five abilities required for managers, supervisors, and workers. This finding remains consistent in nationwide surveys, including those undertaken by the U.S. Department of Labor. The fact that problem-solving skills are so important should not surprise us at all. Organizations need more than information to function successfully. They depend on people who have the ability to transform this information into creative solutions that produce results. Problem solving is a major part of that work.

Given the importance of problem solving, numerous books and resources have been written on the topic. Some address specific types of problems, such as how to build an effective team, create a strategic plan, or design an information system. Others focus on problem solving in a specific field, such as human resources, marketing, strategic planning, or operations. *The Solution Path* is unique among them in that it provides step-by-step instructions and how-to exercises for addressing a variety of problems in different fields. It also offers an approach that will help you enhance your own problem-solving effectiveness as well as increase the potential of your team to create and implement innovative solutions. Perhaps most importantly, it will show you how to keep moving toward your goals even when things seem impossible.

The innovative approach to problem solving that I have developed in *The Solution Path* is based on my own cross-disciplinary education in engineering and the behavioral sciences, as well as my two decades of experience helping top executives at hundreds of companies to find creative solutions and achieve their objectives in a manner that is efficient, timely, and cost-effective. This book draws together the best problem-solving practices I have encountered in my work. More importantly, *The Solution Path* aims to demystify and disseminate best practices from both engineering and the behavioral sciences so that you can use them to improve your workplace and to enhance your own problem-solving skills at the same time.

A unique aspect of this book's problem-solving methodology is that it capitalizes on and maximizes your repositories of positive thinking and creativity. It puts the emphasis on bringing out the best in yourself and your team. It starts by helping you visualize ideal outcomes to your situation and come up with as many ideas as possible, then synthesize them into the best workable solution, and then take action. This is quite different from the usual emphasis of conventional problem solving, which starts by focusing on the problem and analyzing the causes before moving on to evaluating alternatives and taking action. The technique of starting with possibilities rather than analysis has been proved to lead to innovative results, as evidenced by experts such as Gerald Nadler and David Cooperrider, professor at Case Western Reserve University.

The Solution Path offers much more than theory. This book is designed to help you take direct action on a current challenge. As shown in Figure I.1, each chapter starts with *concepts*, quickly translates them into *methods* and *tools*, and then moves on to *exercises* that guide you through a series of concrete steps for turning a challenge into a winning solution. In short, *The Solution Path* is an inspirational learning and action-oriented experience. You will return to it again and again as you bring each new problem to the drawing board.

Figure I.1 The Road Map for Each Chapter

Who Should Read This Book

The problem-solving approach I offer here is applicable to organizations in a wide range of fields and functions, from human resources to engineering, from strategic planning to product development. Executives and managers will find the book helpful for addressing a host of work-related challenges, such as devising and implementing new strategies, building a solid and coherent team, redesigning a facility, implementing a new information system, and motivating employees, to name only a few. Newly promoted supervisors and managers, who immediately feel the weight of having to produce results through inspiring and motivating their employees, will find the book particularly useful because of its emphasis on working synergistically with individuals and groups to solve problems. Individual employees will also benefit from reading the book, as it will instruct them in taking initiative, using creativity techniques, working successfully with peers and managers, and contributing effectively to teams. Whatever your challenge, your organization, or your position, *The Solution Path* will inspire you to jump-start and sustain your problem-solving activities, and create lasting change.

What's Inside

The Solution Path presents a set of proven methods that are used by successful people when they approach problems. Every chapter includes numerous cases that illustrate key concepts and tools. Although these cases reflect real-life examples, all names and particulars have been disguised. Any similarity to real names and circumstances is purely coincidental. The first four chapters are devoted to establishing the fundamental cornerstones underlying effective problem solving: positive thinking, working effectively with individuals and teams, and facilitation. The next four chapters then detail the major steps of the problem-solving process, namely, envisioning outcomes, developing ideas, formulating solutions, and taking action.

More specifically, Chapter One, "Getting Started," gives you the basic outlines of the problem-solving methodology that will be elaborated on in the rest of the book. It also gets you thinking about which of your present challenges you may want to use as your "test case" for problem solving as we proceed through the action exercises offered in each chapter.

Chapter Two, "Positive Thinking," looks at the main factor that impedes most people from acting on their problems: fear. This chapter helps you understand the root causes behind fear and allows you to identify its many facets, including denial, doubt, resisting change, and searching for blame. It also provides you with techniques for engaging in positive thinking and transforming fear into action.

The most important asset for creating opportunities—people— is the focus of Chapter Three, "Working with Individuals and Teams." This chapter provides you with an understanding of the dynamics of effective relationships, as well as information on how to build a team to solve your problem. Chapter Four, "Group Facilitation," then provides you with techniques to help that team maximize its time together throughout its problem-solving efforts. It outlines the basics of facilitation, providing a set of methods for solving problems in a group environment and a means of building effective teams.

Chapter Five, "Starting with a Clear Vision," shows you why it is important to begin any problem-solving process with a strong vision of an ideal outcome and then provides you with a set of principles and tools that your team can use to develop a vision for your particular challenge. In Chapter Six, "Creating Ideas," your team is guided to transform its vision into a portfolio of projects from which it will choose one to start. Team members choose a project that is feasible, solves the original problem, promises maximum results, and gets them closer to their vision. Team members then engage both individually and together in a number of techniques to generate ideas for the first project, such as association and free association, using metaphors, asking "what if" questions, taking breaks, consulting dreams, establishing deadlines, visualization, and brainstorming.

How to sort through and combine these ideas into something workable is the topic of Chapter Seven, "Developing the Solution." Your team will learn how to prioritize, come up with alternatives, combine alternatives into complete solutions, select the best solution by using consensus, and then further refine the solution. Chapter Eight, "Taking Action," guides your team in designing a step-by-step action plan for making the solution a reality. It also helps the group factor in potential risks, communicate the solution to others, plan the transition to the new solution, evaluate the solution, and make future improvements.

The Conclusion encourages you to see your current challenges as part of a broader life journey in which problems serve as lessons that lead not only to organizational improvements but also to personal fulfillment and growth.

Spiritual Principles Underlying This Book

Another characteristic that separates *The Solution Path* from other books on problem solving is its reliance on a few basic spiritual principles. Although these principles do not produce results by themselves, they can give you an enormous creative edge in problem solving when they are used in conjunction with the book's practical methods and tools. They also fuel you with optimism to continue working on your problems even when things may feel gloomy. I have come to witness the power of these principles time and time again in my personal and professional life.

One such principle is the idea that our greatest ally in solving problems is our Higher Power. I use the term Higher Power because of its universality across different faiths. You may choose to believe in this Higher Power in whatever form you prefer. This book is based on the premise that our Higher Power does indeed exist and provides us with support and resources. I will draw on this idea in various ways throughout the book as a means of assisting you in problem solving.

A second principle is the idea that the universe is inherently an abundant place in which all of the resources we need to solve problems—time, people, money, and ideas—are available to us in unlimited quantities. In other words, we are all part of an infinite pie, a pie that never runs out of pieces. Believing that abundance, rather than scarcity, is the order of the day and is available to everyone is a powerful force in helping us have trust and faith in any problem-solving process. It helps us shift out of fear-based behavior and a kind of "hoarding" mentality and allows us to trust that what we need will ultimately be there. This gives us the opportunity to expand our thinking in unlimited ways. Unlimited thinking consequently enables our true creativity to flourish. Under such expansive conditions, our solutions ultimately become much more effective and successful.

A third principle is that we can use our conscious mind to affect reality in ways that we do not fully comprehend. Simply by putting thoughts out into the world, we are already influencing the course of events. Therefore, if we want to create positive situations in our lives, it is very important that we keep our thoughts positive and constructive. In a world in which complaining is a favorite pastime and despair can, through habit, be a more familiar friend than hope, this sometimes requires great discipline. Positive thinking is particularly important in the problem-solving process, as it is a key element in helping us move toward constructive solutions. Techniques for engaging in positive thinking will therefore be an important part of this book.

Do you want to turn your challenges around? Are you ready to shoot for the stars? If so, let's begin.

Chapter One

Getting Started

First say to yourself what you would be;
and then do what you have to do.

—Epictetus

"Our team can be a lot more effective. But no matter how much I try, I can't seem to get team members to agree on our core objectives so that we all pull in the same direction."

"Our company is downsizing, and I have to make recommendations for layoffs. I feel so numb! I don't know where to start, but I have to make decisions this weekend."

"We just spent two years installing a new information system. So much effort and so much money! But instead of benefits, we're getting more customer complaints than last year."

"We must get to a different level with operations, or we will start losing customers to the competition. Our product quality is consistent, but we keep missing our delivery dates."

Every day we face new problems. At work, at home, in our communities, and everywhere, problems are part of our path. What is it for you today?

Expanding your business

Downsizing

Laying off employees

Creating a new product line

Implementing a strategic plan

Relocating the organization

Dealing with high turnover

Losing a valuable employee

Reorganizing the company

Installing a new information technology system

Creating a learning organization

Building a team

Dealing with difficult team members

The list of challenges we potentially face at work is endless. If you want to start addressing them, you have come to the right place. Simply by picking up this book, you have taken the first step along the "solution path." This book does not promise to give you expert answers to each and every one of the situations listed, nor does it promise to make all of your problems go away. But it will provide you with a methodology that you can apply to problems across the board. This methodology will allow you to capitalize on your own potential and the capabilities of your team.

This chapter will get you started by giving you the outlines of that methodology. It will also help you consider which of your present problems you may want to address as we proceed through the book.

Problem Solving in Action: The Mailing House

The best way to get a sense of the methodology I will be presenting here is to look at an example of how one company was able to solve a serious problem successfully.

Delores was the president and owner of the Mailing House, a company dedicated to doing mass mailings for a variety of clients. Over a ten-year period, she built her organization from a five-person operation functioning out of her garage to a fifty-employee company with its own facility. Eventually she landed a huge contract with a major grocery chain, which brought the company to a completely new level. Delores hired her colleague, James, as the new vice president of operations, and within one year, the company doubled in size and was operating in a redesigned facility.

Then trouble hit. A national retail chain bought out the grocery client, and the Mailing House's contract was not renewed.

At first, Delores and James spent hours and hours trying to figure out why this had happened to them. They focused on coming up with tactics to contact the new ownership and regain the account. But they were not successful. After four months, they had to lay off five employees. And their fears about the potential failure of their business started spreading to their staff.

Dolores was shaken but not defeated. She decided to stop focusing on the lost account. Instead, she would concentrate on creating new opportunities. She and James called a companywide meeting to try to harness the energies of the group. The two leaders discussed their vision and their ideal picture of what a successful resolution of their current crisis might look like. With the help of the team, they generated several ideas for fulfilling their vision. They organized their thoughts into a solid solution that was acceptable to all participants. They then devised a step-by-step action plan to implement their solution. Within six months, the Mailing House had many new accounts and a new product that they had created for existing and new clients: office supplies. They were on their way.

The Methods of the Solution Path

Delores's success in overcoming her challenge began with her decision to stop focusing on the company's current problem—losing its major client—and to move from fear to positive action. Her next successful move was to call on the collective energy of her employees in the solution effort and engage in effective facilitation to come up with strategies and action steps to help them get out of their bind.

Thus Delores built her solution process on the very principles that form what I call the cornerstones of this book's approach to problem solving:

1. Thinking positively is essential for addressing challenges.

2. Working with individuals and teams is imperative for creating solutions.

3. Employing effective facilitation is critical for harnessing group energies successfully.

These cornerstones are key to finding the solution to any problem. Positive thinking inspires you and others to begin and continue your work on problems, despite the difficulties you may encounter. Involving others allows you to multiply the amount of creative thinking that can be applied to the situation at hand. And working with others effectively through skilled facilitation lets you maximize the time spent on the problem.

Delores and her team also engaged in four major steps that serve as the backbone to the methodology that will be fleshed out in this book, namely:

1. Envisioning your ideal outcome

2. Creating ideas for solutions

3. Sorting and synthesizing ideas into a holistic solution

4. Developing a step-by-step action plan and implementing the solution

Figure 1.1 illustrates this four-step problem-solving methodology and the three cornerstones on which it rests. As the figure indicates, the parts of the process involving "envisioning" and "creating ideas" make up the "expansion" phase of problem solving. The main questions you will be addressing at this stage are "What would our situation look like if things were ideal?" and "How many different ideas can we come up with for moving toward that outcome?" This phase has to do with broadening your horizons and thinking big. This means that believing rather than doubting must be your best ally during these two steps. Believing means that all ideas, all possibilities, need to be considered.

The parts of the process involving "developing the solution" and "taking action" make up the "consolidation" phase of problem solving. During this phase, you play the "doubting game" while still continuing to believe that things will work out in the end. Your main questions in this phase become "Does this solution work?" "Does it take into account the most serious risks?" and "How can we make things work?" You take a more critical look at your options, narrow them down and combine them where appropriate, and make concrete short- and long-term plans to turn your situation around.

Whereas in an ideal world these steps would be sequential, in practice they are usually not. Often you will find that you'll need to go back and forth between them. For example, you may have decided to expand your production volumes based on higher product demand levels. Yet by the time you get to the stage of developing

Figure 1.1 Methods of the Solution Path

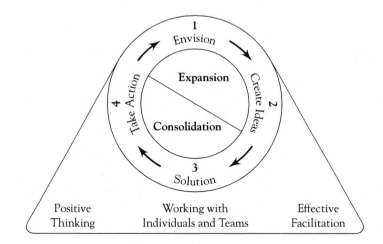

the solution, the external parameters of your situation (for example, the economy) may change dramatically, resulting in lower product demand levels. This will force you to go back to the first step, in which you must create a new vision for your situation. Or you may be working on reducing product costs. You may be at the stage of taking action when a team member comes up with a much better idea, which has to be incorporated. This will take you back to stage 2 of the process. The steps of this problem-solving methodology, then, function together as part of an iterative process in which data from a later stage may need to be brought back to an earlier stage and reworked.

Action Exercises

Let us now begin to take action on the challenges you yourself are facing. This is the first of many exercises that I provide to help you apply the principles of the book to your own work situation. To utilize these exercises most effectively, I strongly recommend that you write down or type your responses. This will help you organize your thoughts and come to new insights. You may want to establish a separate notebook for this task or record your notes in a computer document.

Given that most organizational solutions are the result of group efforts, my recommendation is that after you create your problem-solving team in Chapter Three, you also come back to this chapter to complete the activities with that team. Keeping a progress log for your team as you move toward developing and implementing your solutions may be useful in this regard. If you maintain your log in a three-ring binder, for example, you can include both the results of these exercises and notes from your meetings as a team.

The first exercise in this chapter tests your readiness to embrace your current problems and to start creating opportunities. The second exercise asks you to articulate what you believe are your most crucial workplace challenges.

Exercise 1.1: Opportunity Readiness Questionnaire

1. Are you sick of feeling stuck because of your current work problems?

2. Are you tired of complaining about your present work problems?

3. Are you spending a lot of time analyzing why your problems exist?

4. Do you find that you're spending a lot of time wishing things were different?

5. Has your work environment stopped energizing you and your team members or colleagues?

6. Do you find that you are underutilizing your potential or that your team or colleagues are?

7. Are you imagining endless "what if" scenarios to predict what could happen to you if you acted one way or another on these problems?

8. Do you find that you are postponing taking action until tomorrow?

9. Do you feel capable of creating change if you had the right help?

Did you answer yes to at least three questions in Exercise 1.1? That means you are ready to start creating opportunities out of your current problems.

Exercise 1.2: Identifying Your Major Work Problems

Think of three current work challenges, important issues that you need to resolve and are dealing with daily. Although some of them might overlap and be part of a larger overall problem, try to articulate three discrete situations. Write them down.

Problem 1

Problem 2

Problem 3

Which is the most important for you to solve?

Which is the most difficult for you to solve?

Which seems to have the most possibilities for resolution?

If you had to address only one, which would you start with?

At this point, perhaps you are already beginning to recognize that your problems can also be seen as opportunities for change. Chapter Two will take you much further in this direction. It will help you start analyzing your fears about your challenges and will empower you to take positive action. Let's continue along the solution path.

Chapter Two

Positive Thinking:
From Fear to Action

We can easily forgive a child who is afraid of the dark.
The real tragedy of life is when men are afraid of the light.

—Plato

Do you feel stuck and unable to take action on the work situation that you identified in Chapter One even though you know it needs to change? What is it that prevents you from starting to work on this problem?

In this chapter, you will learn about the power of positive thinking in the problem-solving process. You will find out about the detrimental role that fear plays and the way it manifests for you, your colleagues, your subordinates, and your superiors. You'll come to identify your own fears, and you will put together a toolbox for staying positive and taking action on your problems.

Moving Beyond Fear: Custom Aerodynamics

The following story illustrates how one manager was able to move through his fears and take positive steps that helped his company not only avoid bankruptcy but also diversify its product lines.

Brad was a development engineer for Custom Aerodynamics, a medium-sized firm that specialized in designing and customizing parts for large aerospace companies. He had been promoted three times since starting with the company twelve years earlier, most recently to the position of director of business development.

The aerospace industry had been under tremendous change, and the company was actively looking to obtain new design contracts in order to stay afloat. Six months after Brad's promotion, 80 percent of Custom Aerodynamics' bids were either canceled or lost to the competition. Top management decided to initiate layoffs and a hiring freeze.

Fear began to grip the entire company. Brad's business development department, in particular, which was Custom Aerodynamics' primary engine for new contract generation, was especially susceptible to panic. Brad and his team of engineers felt that it was almost impossible for the company to survive. They spent months discussing the reasons why this was happening to them. Meetings with top executives merely stirred up more fear and led to directives for more bids on the main product line, customized parts. Most of these bids did not materialize.

Brad knew that if the company was to pull through its crisis, it would have to create a new product line: electronics. But top executives seemed ambivalent about the idea. Brad therefore had to grapple with two fears: his fear of going against the grain with top executives and his fear of personal failure should his idea be given a chance but ultimately not succeed.

Brad was able to gain some mastery over his fears simply by starting to take action. He talked with every development engineer in his department and in the company as a whole about his idea. In doing so, he gathered information that indicated that the potential for diversification in the company was great. And the more he took action, the more positive he felt. Working with five other engineers, Brad put together a presentation on creating an electronics product line that would capitalize on the strengths of an aerospace supplier that Custom Aerodynamics had recently acquired.

When Brad enthusiastically announced this plan to the company's executive team, however, he received only a lukewarm response. While the president of the company and the vice president of marketing and sales (his boss) were encouraging, the chief financial officer expressed serious doubts about the proposal.

Brad considered this reaction a small setback. Taking action had filled him with positive thinking and conviction about the potential of this new product line. By continuing to work on the project, coming up with specific ideas for new contracts and bids, and communicating his efforts to the company's executive team in a professional and enthusiastic fashion, he was eventually able to convince management to approve his group's idea. Brad and his team then designed an action plan to bring their idea to fruition.

Their first step was to take their presentation and turn it into a marketing brochure. They then used this brochure to pitch the electronics line to the company's existing client base. Although they were still apprehensive about whether their plan would succeed or not, they found that taking steps on their action plan helped them quell their fears. As they actively looked for new contracts, they felt even better. Within a few months, Brad and his team were sitting in their first meeting for a new contract in electronics. Production of the new line began soon thereafter.

The Answer: Positive Thinking

Brad's ultimate success can be attributed in large part to the fact that he was able to maintain a positive attitude throughout the entire proposal process—about himself, his convictions, his potential project, and his team.

The Believing Game

Brad had decided to play what is called the Believing Game. The Believing Game, which was first described by author and former professor Peter Elbow, involves looking at a problem and rather than concentrating on its uncomfortable and negative aspects, thinking, "This is a great opportunity. We can do so much to turn the situation around. We will create something new and exciting."

According to Napoleon Hill, author of *Think and Grow Rich*, believing is synonymous with having faith; he calls it "the chemist of the mind" because it activates chemicals in the brain that help us feel energized and upbeat. By consciously choosing to believe in positive possibilities, we also help our sometimes less cooperative subconscious mind to begin adjusting its thinking as well so that it is less likely to revert to primitive fears and sabotage us in hidden ways. Thus believing propels us to start creating solutions both consciously and subconsciously. In contrast, when we choose to doubt, we focus on why it is so hard and even futile to take action. We stay stuck in our problems. Franklin Roosevelt articulated the contrast between believing and doubting when he stated, "The only limit to our realization of tomorrow will be our doubts of today. Let us move forward with strong and active faith."

The Believing Game is powerful because it is based on a fundamental spiritual law that was related to us by the Buddha: We are what we think. All that we are arises with our thoughts. With our thoughts we make the world. Its corollary is: What you focus on is what you draw to you. Henry Ford, the pioneer of mass automation, showed that he had internalized this law when he said, "If you think you can, or if you think you can't, you are right."

So if "you are what you think," it's clear that if you want to be successful, your thoughts had better be positive.

Opportunities, Not Problems

Scientific findings overwhelmingly confirm the power of positive thinking. As Robert Sutton, a professor at Stanford University, has observed, more than five hundred research studies affirm that positive thinking is one of the most significant factors leading to innovative solutions. In 1988, the *Harvard Business Review* published an article titled "Pygmalion in Management." Pygmalion was a mythological sculptor who created the statue of a beautiful woman. He believed so strongly that this statue could come to life that the goddess Venus eventually granted him his wish. As a result, the statue became his wife, Galitea. The *Review* article illustrated how the "Pygmalion effect" occurs in the business world all the time: When managers believe strongly that their subordinates will perform effectively, those subordinates do, in fact, live up to the managers' expectations. The converse is also true: When managers believe that their subordinates will not perform well, those subordinates prove to be ineffective.

And let us not forget the power of the "placebo effect." Medical research consistently reveals that a certain percentage of study participants who are given nothing but sugar pills but think they have been given a new drug to combat their condition respond as though they have actually taken medicine! The mind is powerful indeed, more powerful than most of us probably realize.

The annals of history are filled with stories of people who were able to defy the odds and succeed in bringing something new into the world only by rigorously maintaining an attitude of positive thinking. When President Kennedy articulated the dream of landing a man on the moon and bringing him back safely, who would have believed it possible? Yet Kennedy persisted in his vision, and within a few years, the impossible became a reality. On the business front, call to mind any of the pioneers who have brought innovative products and services to market, and you will have an example of the power of positive thinking. Steve Jobs at Apple Computer, for instance, was able to overcome doubts and setbacks to produce the Macintosh computer, an innovation that caused a huge shift in the entire personal computer industry.

If you believe in a Higher Power, you have an added advantage in problem solving, because calling on that Higher Power can aid and enhance your ability to stay on the positive-thinking track. I have found this to be true in the business world and in my own life.

For example, when I completed my doctoral degree, with an emphasis on the management of organizational change and innovation, the U.S. economy was facing a severe downturn, and unemployment levels were skyrocketing. Most of my colleagues and I felt terrified to step into the workforce at a time of such economic instability. Some of my peers decided to continue their studies rather than venture out into the turmoil, and I also seriously considered taking that path. But I continually asked my Higher Power for guidance and as a result was inspired to focus on working with the very kinds of clients that were most needing of services in a bad economy: those who faced the need to downsize or to break into new markets. As a result, I had the wonderful opportunity of partnering with dozens of companies, assisting them in implementing changes that would reenergize their organizations. In addition, I used my knowledge of product development and innovation to create retraining programs for engineering professionals who had become unemployed and were looking to found new high-technology companies.

Clearly, the way you choose to perceive problems makes a big difference in how successful you are at solving them. You can look at them as negative occurrences that are preventing you from going forward, or you can look at them as situations that are providing opportunities to advance along the path. Would you rather experience your work life as one long string of problems or one long string of opportunities? The sooner you are able to stop fighting problems and embrace them as chances for learning and change, the sooner you will be able to start addressing them constructively.

Positive thinking can therefore pave the way for breakthrough changes in your professional life. Yet it is common to stay stuck in your present challenges. What are the most serious barriers that hinder you from advancing your teams, departments, and organizations? How can you overcome those barriers?

Fear: The Major Stumbling Block

There are, of course, numerous impediments that keep you stuck in your current situation. But I believe that all of them boil down to one thing: fear.

The first level of fear has to do with concerns as to whether you or your organization have the resources it takes to solve a particular problem, such as time, equipment, people, or money, and the know-how and strength to pull it off. A deeper level of fear, however, has to do with worries about failing and the consequences of such failure to your professional and personal well-being.

Those little voices of fear can concoct quite a disconcerting inner dialogue: "A great project, but do you really think you'll have the time to complete it on top of all your other duties?" "Your business idea is interesting, but are you sure that you'll be successful?" "If you try to implement this project, everyone is going to oppose you. Your colleagues may even become hostile and decide they don't like you anymore. And then they will take sick days or quit, and productivity will suffer. Your department won't meet its goals. You could even be fired!" And sometimes you'll hear these voices reflected by others as well, which tends to give them extra potency.

These negative voices can lead you into dangerous dungeons of imaginary despair and tragedy. They keep you from taking action. In short, fear prolongs problems and solves none.

The Many Faces of Fear

Fear can disguise itself and manifest itself in many different ways. Let us look at a few of the many forms of fear that operate overtly or covertly in relation to various problems within an organization. Recognizing the faces of fear is an important step toward dispelling them so that you can move on to finding and implementing solutions.

Denial. Sometimes when problems hit, particularly if they are large, complex, and overwhelming, one's first response is to deny that such challenges exist. Denying the very existence of negative conditions means that everyone can live under the illusion for a while that things are OK and that no effort needs to be exerted to make changes. I have seen leaders, managers, and entire organizations remain in complete denial over some very serious situations. Yet we all know that denial can go on for only so long. In one way or another, problems will eventually scream to be addressed. And the longer problems are neglected, the larger and thornier they tend to become.

I still recall, for instance, meeting the chief executive and owner of a defense-related corporation. Even though his company was in serious financial trouble because defense contracts were drying up, he still did not see the urgency of diversifying into commercial fields. Because he stayed in complete denial, he was forced to lay off all of his employees and declare bankruptcy.

Resisting Change. Most people prefer the known to the unknown because the known offers at least some semblance of security and safety, whereas the unknown may involve risk. Hence organizations—and most individuals in organizations—tend to be reluctant to address problems because doing so inevitably involves change.

But let's break this down a bit further. As professor and author Andrew Van de Ven notes, people resist change when they don't have a clear picture of what it involves or will lead to, it is imposed on them, it means they will lose something of benefit to them, and it interferes with their current priorities.

Consider what happened at a school district that decided to upgrade its accounting, purchasing, and payroll systems by adopting a series of SAP software systems. Even though these systems had proved helpful in the corporate world in automating and handling information effectively, the school district did not achieve good results. Why? District employees were not consulted in designing the system, nor were they offered the information they needed to perceive the benefits. True to human nature, they resisted the change and continued to use the various old systems for more than a year after the SAP systems were installed. They eventually formed a special task force to turn the situation around.

Furthermore, fear about change translates into anxiety in the workplace, which in turn leads to absenteeism and turnover. It also spells delays in implementing large-scale programs, such as the installation of a new information system or a new management structure. Ultimately, resistance to change results in a loss of productivity, with negative consequences on sales and revenues.

Doubting. Sometimes the reluctance to address workplace problems comes down to people's doubts about their own or others' ability to address the situation appropriately and create new opportunities. What this ultimately comes down to is a fear of failure.

For example, the director of a local printing plant was doubtful about the abilities of his employees to switch to a completely automated system that would double the plant's productivity. He was therefore afraid he would fail to make change happen, so he dragged his heels on implementing the new system. The result was lost sales and delays in deliveries. Finally, the company's chief executive had to intervene, and the plant was completely overhauled. It took about year to complete the installation, but the results were spectacular.

Placing Blame. A couple of years ago, I was invited by the director of a customer service department that was receiving serious client complaints. After talking with the director and a few key players, I could see that the department was focusing on blaming everyone else for the problems that customers were having. According to department employees, the front office was at fault because it did not forward customer calls promptly. The information systems department was to blame for the inefficiencies of the order tracking system. Sales employees were promising the impossible. Everyone was at fault and needed to take corrective action—except the customer service department.

This is what happens when fear leads people to blame others about their own shortcomings. There are always numerous people and events on which we can cast blame for our current situations: bosses, coworkers, subordinates, the economy, and so on. The blame game can be endless. Although it may provide temporary relief by lifting responsibility for your situation off your shoulders for a while, it is ultimately a waste of time and a flimsy excuse for taking no action.

The flip side of this is to relentlessly blame yourself for what-ever mess you are facing. You may chastise yourself over and over for having made a mistake that led to the present situation, for not having had the foresight to see trouble coming, for not having taken the initiative to learn a new skill that would have prevented the problem, and so forth. It is certainly true that accepting re-sponsibility for your actions is to be commended. But beating your-self up is, like blaming others, a waste of time and prevents you from starting to create opportunities that will allow you to move beyond the problem.

Identifying Your Own Fears

The following exercises ask you to think about your fears about previous and current challenges. Please take the time to com-plete them in a thoughtful manner. Once you have created your problem-solving team in Chapter Three, you may want to return to these exercises and have your team members complete them as well.

Exercise 2.1: Identifying Fears About a Previous Challenge

Think about a serious problem you encountered that was resolved in a way that dramatically changed your job or your organization.

Describe your challenge.

Describe your initial reaction to the problem.

List your top five worst fears at the time about this situation.

1.

2.

3.

4.

5.

Describe the final outcome of this situation.

Describe whether any of your worst fears materialized. If they did, discuss how you resolved them.

Describe how you now look upon the situation.

List the top three lessons you learned from this problem.

1.

2.

3.

Exercise 2.2: Identifying Fears About a Current Challenge

Review the most important of your three current problems from Exercise 1.2 at the end of Chapter One.

List the top five fears you have about taking action on this problem.

1.

2.

3.

4.

5.

Have you already started working on your current problem? If so, describe the action steps you have taken.

If you have already started working on your problem, are your fears still with you? Have they increased or have they diminished?

If you have not started working on your challenge, have your fears increased or decreased now that you have clearly identified them?

Most Fears Don't Come True

So what is the verdict? Did your fears materialize in the past? What were your lessons if they did? Have you started taking action on your current challenge? Has doing so helped your fears begin to diminish?

If you have begun to take action on your problem, most likely you're finding that your fears are lessening. As psychologist and fear expert Susan Jeffers states in *Feel the Fear and Do It Anyway*, our most negative and hidden worries have only a 10 percent chance of coming true. This means that 90 percent of your most serious fears never actually materialize. And indeed, my personal and professional experience working with executives at hundreds of companies has confirmed that even in the most adverse situations, the scariest speculations hardly ever become realities.

But let's take the worst-case scenario. What if your deepest fears did come to pass? What if the most horrible thing of all happened—you utterly and miserably failed?

Well, let's look at your past challenge. If your fears materialized, what did you learn? What do you think you might learn if your worst fears materialize in your present circumstance?

The Center for Creative Leadership is a leading international organization based in North Carolina that focuses on enhancing the effectiveness of leaders and managers worldwide. Its research has shown that despite the great difficulties we may experience as a result of our biggest problems, in most situations these difficulties allow us to learn and break through to new paths. The center's findings based on research with hundreds of individuals remain consistent: *successful leaders learn the most and make the greatest strides in their careers when they face challenges—and even hardships*. Challenges and hardships include difficulties like yours: impossible bosses, coworkers, and employees; terrible job assignments; downsizing; and so-called mistakes and failures.

Remember the example mentioned earlier of Steve Jobs and the legendary Macintosh computer? Well, the Macintosh would not have happened had it not been for an earlier failure, the Lisa computer. Lisa was also very innovative, but it was expensive and did not sell well. Yet Apple learned from its Lisa lessons and forged ahead. And the Macintosh was a triumph.

In an article in the *Harvard Business Review* titled "Inspiring Innovation," Michael Dell, the founder and CEO of Dell Computer described how his company learned from a major disaster it experienced when the computer industry was transitioning to using a new memory chip. Dell was forced to switch over to using the new chip, which left the company stuck with a huge inventory of an older type of memory chip. It took about a year to recover from the resulting financial loss, but the lessons learned led Dell to develop new ways of managing inventory that ended up putting it far ahead of the competition.

Thomas Edison, one of the world's greatest inventors, similarly faced trials and tribulations. Yet he was able to keep going by framing his so-called failures in a constructive way. His motto was "I have not failed. I've just found ten thousand ways that won't work."

In sum, your fears usually do not materialize. And even when they do, they lead to lessons that help you get to a new level of success. In other words, even if your fears are realistic, you must not allow them to hinder you from starting to resolve a challenge. Instead, you must take action, because, as Susan Jeffers says, only by doing so will you find your fears starting to dissipate. If nothing else, putting all of your nervous energy into taking active steps certainly beats sitting around feeling helpless and worried.

Positive Action

Now that you have a better understanding of both the power of positive thinking and the role of fear in problem solving, it's time to take positive action. Let's begin to create what I call your Positive Action Toolbox (see Exhibit 2.1). Doing so will provide you with a foundation of confidence that will then allow you to step up and be a voice of leadership in your organization for solving the workplace problem that you identified in Chapter One.

Again, once you have assembled your problem-solving team in Chapter Three, you may want to return to this chapter and have each of your team members complete the following exercises. This will further empower your group to begin addressing the challenge at hand.

Taking Your Positive Inventory

To fortify yourself for positive action, it's important to begin by taking stock of what you currently have going for you. This list is what I call your Positive Inventory. It consists of your skills, experience,

---

Exhibit 2.1 Your Positive Action Toolbox

1. Taking your Positive Inventory

2. Imagining what you'd do if you weren't afraid

3. Acting as if you've already created your opportunity

4. Thinking abundantly

5. Repeating affirmations

6. Going inward

7. Surrounding yourself with upbeat people

8. Reading positive-oriented books

---

positive qualities (such as persistence or creativity), allies, and any external factors that are working in your favor. Doing this exercise as early as possible in the problem-solving process serves to reprogram your "wiring" and fills you with a "can do" attitude. It makes you believe in yourself, appreciate the people around you as assets, and begin to see that the situation you are in can really work *for* you and not against you.

It's also good to do this exercise even after you've started working on a problem and are well on the road to opportunity. The roller-coaster nature of problem-related events, as well as the mundane aspects of everyday living, can work to drain our energy. It's sometimes easy to forget our own goodness, the goodness of those around us, and our greater purpose. It's also easy to forget that our Higher Power is there to support us. Periodically taking your Positive Inventory can help you remember all of these things and can serve to recharge your batteries.

It may be helpful for you first to vent your frustrations over your current challenge. Simply write your thoughts down as they come to mind without any editing. This technique is used by organizational change specialists and therapists. It will help transition you into what Kurt Lewin calls the "unfreezing" part of change, the time that any system interested in transforming itself must devote to letting go of its old ways and getting ready for the next steps. Change specialists and therapists first allow the audience or client to complain until the group or person has gotten everything out. Eventually, the storm dissipates and is followed by a phase of constructive problem solving. You'll find that the same will happen for you once you write down all of your negative thoughts and feelings about your current problem. After a while, you'll probably begin to notice that even though your situation may still feel quite challenging, some of your issues may not seem as intimidating as they once did. At that point, you will be ready to move on to your Positive Inventory.

Exercise 2.3: Venting Your Frustrations

Spend fifteen to twenty minutes of uninterrupted time typing or writing out all of your frustrations, complaints, and negative feelings about your most pressing work problem. Do not pause, and do not edit what comes out. Simply record everything that comes to mind. How do you feel now that you have gotten it all out? Did any new insights come to you in the process?

Exercise 2.4: Taking Your Positive Inventory

Take some time to carefully list absolutely everything that is going your way. This includes all of the following:

- Your skills
- Professional experience, knowledge, and wisdom you have acquired
- Your positive personal qualities

- Professional and personal accomplishments
- Support and love you receive from colleagues, friends, and family members
- Allies
- People you could contact or call on for assistance within or outside your organization
- Your Higher Power
- Factors that are working in your favor (such as economic conditions, the acquisition of a new client, or a managerial mandate to improve something within your organization)
- Knowledge and insights you have today about your job and your life that you did not have a year ago

When you have completed this exercise, list as many things about the problem at hand that strike you as positive. You should be able to find at least three positive elements, no matter how small.

Imagining What You'd Do If You Weren't Afraid

Think about Exercise 2.2, in which you listed the top five fears you have about taking action on your current problem. Now remember that 90 percent of our worst fears never come true. If, for a moment, you could suspend your fears, knowing that they are fairly unrealistic anyway, how would this change the manner in which you approached your current problem?

The answers to that question comprise the second item in your Positive Action Toolbox.

Exercise 2.5: What Would You Do If You Were Not Afraid?

Think again of your most pressing challenge. Recall your top five fears about your problem. Now take some time to answer the following questions. Provide a total of at least ten different action items.

What actions would you consider taking if you were not afraid?

What risks might you take?

To whom would you turn for assistance?

What new insights do you have about your problem as a result of writing these things down?

Acting As If You've Already Created Your Opportunity

Once you have energized yourself by taking your Positive Inventory and you have determined the kinds of actions you need to take despite your fears, the next thing you need to add to your toolbox is the "acting as if" item. This involves acting as if your challenge were resolved.

This is what Brad and his team did at Custom Aerodynamics, for example. They started talking to clients as if their new product line were already in place. Their enthusiasm led them to their first contract. You can do the same no matter what your problem. Say that you are faced with customer complaints and you wish to improve customer satisfaction dramatically. You can start acting as if customer satisfaction were already excellent. This would involve behaving in a professional manner while paying special attention and resolving client concerns and problems.

Exercise 2.6: Acting As If

Think about your situation and what you want to accomplish. Now assume that it is already accomplished. How would you act if that were the case?

Name two or three things you can do to start acting as if you've already accomplished your goals.

Thinking Abundantly

As you may recall from the Introduction, the spiritual principle of abundance holds that the universe provides us in plentiful fashion with all of the resources we need to solve problems. Adopting an attitude of abundant thinking is thus yet another powerful tool for staying positive during the problem-solving process. By embracing this concept, by setting out the thought form that the world is filled with everything we need, we establish a powerful intentional field that operates to manifest that reality in sometimes miraculous ways. This process is furthermore one that builds on itself, creating a positive spiral that can infuse you and your team with hope, trust, energy, and enthusiasm for any problem-solving project.

Repeating Affirmations

Affirmations are positive statements that you tailor to your particular situation and repeat over and over to yourself in order to reprogram your subconscious mind. They are always stated in the present tense in order to give your subconscious mind the message that they are already true. Once your mind begins to receive such messages, it goes to work manifesting them into reality in mysterious but powerful ways.

Here are some examples of affirmations:

- We are exceeding our sales targets every month.
- We have installed the best computer system possible.
- This month our customers are more satisfied with our service than ever.
- We are working cooperatively as a team.
- We have all the funding we need to solve our problem.
- We have all the expertise we need to solve our problem.

It is helpful to set aside some time each day for repeating your affirmations. The more often you can feel the truth of such statements, the more likely it is that these statements will manifest as reality for you. It's also a good idea to write out your affirmations and tape them to a spot where you will see them frequently during the day in order to reinforce the message. Once you have put together your problem-solving team, you may want to put such affirmations around the department or workroom on large sheets of flipchart paper to keep everyone positive and inspired.

Exercise 2.7: Affirmations

Think about your challenge. Then put together at least three affirmation statements about it. Make certain that they are stated in the present tense as if they are happening or have already happened.

1.

2.

3.

Going Inward

Taking time each day to focus and center yourself is another powerful tool for staying energized and positive. There are a number of techniques for doing so. One is to set aside some quiet time alone, be it in your office or at home, to simply reflect on your situation. Another is to engage in a more formal meditation-type practice in which you find a quiet place, close your eyes, and spend ten to fifteen minutes simply focusing on your breathing and letting go of any thoughts. Yet another is to set up a special prayer time for calling on your Higher Power to assist you in drawing the help and resources you need.

An article in the *Harvard Business Review* titled "Reawakening Your Passion for Work" discussed how top executives are using these very practices, both alone and in groups, as a means of renewing themselves in the workplace. Such activities help you focus and calm your entire system. They thus enable you to look at your situation from a more balanced and more positive perspective. Moreover, they put you in the proper state of mind in which new insights and creative thoughts can emerge.

Surrounding Yourself with Upbeat People

One of the best techniques for maintaining positive thinking is to hang around with optimistic people. At work and home, take care to surround yourself with people who keep reminding you of the endless possibilities before you in confronting any challenge. Avoid "wet blankets" who speak negatively about your viewpoints and opinions in the guise of "being realistic." Such viewpoints are more the reflection of a pessimistic outlook on their part than they are a realistic assessment of the situation.

Reading Positive-Oriented Books

Compile a list of helpful books that uplift your spirit and fill you with enthusiasm and know-how for taking action on your problems. Then make an effort to read them on a consistent basis. In Appendix A, at the back of this book, I list a number of inspirational works that are filled with problem-solving ideas and tools.

This chapter took you from exploring your fears to adopting an attitude of positive thinking so that you can begin to take action on your problems. The next chapter will help you work effectively with others and create problem-solving teams.

Points to Remember

- Positive thinking is a crucial activity for effective problem solvers. Research has demonstrated that it is one of the most important factors for creating innovative solutions.

- Fear is the core impediment to taking action on problems. It can manifest as denial, doubting, resisting change, and placing blame.

- Our worst fears have only a 10 percent change of coming true. Yet even when they do, they lead to important lessons that are necessary for our future success.

- Starting to act on your problems is the best antidote to fear.

- Taking stock of your positive inventory, thinking about what you'd do if you were not afraid, acting as if you've already created the opportunity, thinking abundantly, repeating affirmations, going inward, surrounding yourself with positive people, and consulting positive-oriented books can help you maintain a positive attitude regarding your challenge.

Chapter Three

Working with Individuals
and Teams

He who knows others is wise.
He who knows himself is enlightened.

—*Lao Tzu*

We're all fascinated by business and political leaders—by their power, their success, and their sometimes larger-than-life persona. Rarely, however, do we reflect on the fact that most leaders rely on a cadre of other people to help them solve their problems and maintain their success. Take Thomas Edison, for example. Behind many of his inventions was a team of fourteen hardworking people. They devoted endless hours to turning Edison's ideas into action plans and innovative products.

All great leaders work in partnership with individuals and teams to devise solutions and achieve successful results. In fact, isn't the drive to accomplish what individuals cannot produce on their own the very reason why organizations exist in the first place?

So we need to remind ourselves that we can't afford to be alone in problem solving. The more complex the problems, the greater the number of individuals we need to turn those problems into opportunities. According to Gerald Nadler, involving others is important to effective problem solving for two main reasons:

1. Other people may have expertise, knowledge, and ideas about your situation that you may not have, and they're often more than happy to share that information if given the appropriate opportunity.

2. Those who will be affected by a situation are more likely to embrace the final solution if they have a hand in creating it.

The Power of Teams

Working with teams has proved to be particularly effective in problem solving. Years ago, for example, a printing company hired me to help design the layout for their new building. The president of the company was desperate. The parent organization was requesting that the move be accomplished in three months, and all the president had was an architectural floor plan.

Although I have an engineering background, I had never worked on the layout of a printing plant before. My colleague, however, had done work in this field. I assured the company president that we could complete the design in three weeks if we got everyone involved. I don't think he believed me, but he had no choice. All the other consultants he had interviewed had asked for at least twice the time and much more money than we did!

The president introduced me to the decision makers and the supervisors of the different areas who were players in the project. My colleague and I then held a meeting in which we invited everyone to participate. All the supervisors chose to become part of the core team despite their confusion about how they could contribute. None of them had experience in designing plant layouts either.

During the first three meetings, it was apparent that the team members knew much more about their own areas and their equipment than my colleague or I ever would. We gave them an overview of how to design the facility using a scaled floor plan and paper cutouts of the equipment. Together, we all started brainstorming different ways of laying out the plant. The supervisors loved it. They felt empowered! They were soon ready to start refining the layout in their own areas.

By the end of the second week, we had all agreed on the preliminary design. Team members were unanimous in feeling that by interacting effectively, they had created a solution that was significantly better than their own individual ideas. During the third week, we involved other relevant planners, decision makers, and budget experts in the process. My colleague drew up the final design, which was approved by all decision makers and was submitted to the parent company. The president of the company was thrilled.

Experiences such as this have proved to me that working in teams leads to superior solutions to problems thanks to what I call the *sigma effect:* the concept that what team members create collectively represents much more than the amalgamation, the sum, of their individual ideas. By working together, the supervisors of the printing plant, for instance, not only generated many more suggestions than they would have on their own but also combined them in unexpected and innovative ways. Innovation happens when team members can expand on the diversity of their ideas rather than allow that diversity to divide them. Moreover, working in teams gives all of the parties involved the chance to develop their creativity and sharpen their problem-solving skills. So using teams sets up a win-win situation both for you and your team members. It's no wonder that the *Journal of Management* reports that over 80 percent of companies with more than one hundred employees—and over 90 percent of Fortune 1000 organizations—use teams.

The Stages of Relationships and Groups

Working with other individuals and teams to solve problems is, however, easier said than done. It is a delicate process that requires dedication, patience, and skill. It requires, in short, knowing how to establish effective relationships with others and how to foster relationship development among team members.

Luckily, the research literature offers many helpful insights about group dynamics and group process that we can draw on here.

One of the most useful findings is that relationships and teams go through a sequence of four stages: *forming, storming, norming,* and *performing* (see Figure 3.1):

1. *Forming* involves people getting together and becoming oriented to one another. This stage is generally characterized by happy optimism.

2. *Storming* occurs as individuals begin to realistically assess one another's skills and abilities for addressing the challenge at hand. In this stage, they are also confronted with one another's personal behaviors, attitudes, communication styles, and idiosyncrasies. This stage is typically characterized by conflicts, frustration, and problems.

3. In the *norming* phase, group members address and resolve their interpersonal issues and establish norms regarding appropriate and expected behaviors.

4. Finally, in the *performing* stage, individuals work cooperatively on the task at hand, performing as expected and devising concrete solutions.

What You Will Learn in This Chapter

Clearly, the more quickly your group can move through its forming and storming stages, the faster it will begin to perform and solve problems effectively. The aim of this chapter is thus to help you to take the first important step toward this end—building effective relationships. This will include the following activities:

- Understanding personality types so that you can focus on the best in yourself and others
- Communicating effectively to create trust
- Learning to listen actively to others in order to gather and organize information about them that will help you work with them more effectively

Figure 3.1 Stages and Tools

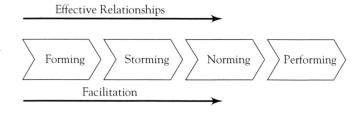

- Identifying the individuals with whom you need to work to solve your problem
- Forming your team

Chapter Four will provide you with the basics for effectively facilitating your problem-solving team.

Building Effective Relationships

Understanding Personality Types and Seeing the Best in Others

Research shows that as complex and unique as each human being is, every person can be categorized according to where he or she falls on four basic personality dimensions. Knowing what "type" you and others are on these dimensions can help you understand yourself and the people you work with more clearly. Consequently, it can provide you with valuable information about how you may work more effectively with even people you find to be the most personally challenging.

The first important point to note is that people's basic personality types remain largely unchanged throughout their lives. This means that your aim in working with others should not be to try to change them. That sort of effort usually results only in conflict, power struggles, and deep scars and rarely yields the results for which you had hoped. I am suggesting that you use the information about personality types instead to understand and accept others the way they are, see the best in them, and recognize that diversity and variety among team members are the keys to innovation.

The Four Personality Dimensions

The system I am using for classifying personalities is drawn from the Myers-Briggs Type Indicator, or MBTI, a test that is based on the work of the pioneering psychologist Carl Jung. The MBTI was created by Katherine Briggs and Isabel Briggs Myers after World War II and provides a reliable and valid instrument for determining personality dimensions. The test identifies four basic dimensions along which each of us can be "typed" in one direction or another. It is important to note that none of the resulting types is "better" than another; each one is equally valid and has its strengths and weaknesses. Typing people, therefore, is a means of gathering information about their natural proclivities; it is not a means of determining people's values or character.

The four basic personality dimensions are these:

- *Extroversion versus introversion:* Preferring crowds or solitude?

- *Sensing versus intuiting:* Using five—or six—senses?

- *Thinking versus feeling:* Operating from the head or the heart?

- *Judging versus perceiving:* Preferring efficiency or flexibility?

Extroversion Versus Introversion: Preferring Crowds or Solitude? Extroverts prefer being with others to being alone. They become energized by relating to and interacting with people. True extroverts are those who go to a party and are excited to meet as many individuals as possible. About 75 percent of the population can be characterized as extroverts.

Introverts, by contrast, feel less comfortable interacting with others and prefer silence and solitude. They recharge their batteries by being alone. Since introverts are in the minority, they often feel uncomfortable and self-conscious. They tend to go through life believing that they need to show more of their extroverted side. If, however, extroverts make introverts feel comfortable for being themselves, introverts can open up and share amazing insights about problems and solutions.

Sensing Versus Intuiting: Using Five—or Six—Senses? Sensing people take in the world and base their understanding of it on what they perceive with their five senses: sight, hearing, touch, taste, and smell. These people love hard-core, nuts-and-bolts data and can only relate to proven theories. Intuitives instead like to perceive and make sense of the world using their "sixth sense"— their intuition—rather than just their five senses. They look beyond proven theories and facts to consider the big picture, broader concepts, and what could be rather than what is. Most individuals, 75 percent, are sensing types, which explains why the business world is primarily ruled by facts and data.

Sensing and intuitive types can come into serious conflict during problem solving. So it is important that you and all of the members of your team recognize that each type brings its own strengths to the table and that working together will lead you to better and more innovative solutions than if only one type were present. Indeed, the first two steps of the Solution Path—envisioning and creating ideas—rely primarily on the contributions of intuitive types who can engage in creative, "right-brain" thinking. The second two steps of the Solution Path—developing the solution and taking action—require the skills of sensing types, who are better at sticking to brass tacks and formulating concrete options.

Thinking Versus Feeling: Operating from the Head or the Heart? Thinking types like to make objective decisions based on logic and reason. Feeling types prefer to make decisions based on emotional and personal considerations—in particular, they are concerned with how their decisions will personally affect other people.

While formal schooling and our culture at large tend to emphasize the thinking rather than feeling functions in decision making, the population is split evenly between the two types. These two types of people can work in a complementary fashion, particularly when they appreciate the two different ways of making decisions. This means that feeling types need to understand that thinking types have deep emotions but are driven by rational thinking. Thinking types, on the other hand, need to realize that feeling types think logically but don't always verbalize their reasoning. Once team members of each type develop an appreciation for the other type, all will come to see that their decisions do indeed benefit from having differing viewpoints present.

Judging Versus Perceiving: Preferring Efficiency or Flexibility? Individuals who like to plan and schedule their time diligently, stick to deadlines, and come to closure about decisions as quickly as possible are known as judging types. Perceiving types, by contrast, are fans of flexibility and openness. They keep their schedules somewhat loose, like to toss around lots of ideas without necessarily settling on any of them, and may set deadlines as alarms for *starting* rather than finishing projects. The population is split evenly between judging and perceiving types.

Understandably, these two types can come into considerable conflict in working with each other. Perceivers may think that judgers are rigid, while judgers may think that perceivers are ineffectual. But having both types on your team can be helpful. Perceiving types might be more available to you and others because they keep their schedules open. They are also willing to consider new ideas and possibilities up until the last minute, which can be helpful in situations that require a great deal of flexibility and creativity. Judging types are trusty and reliable. You know that if you schedule a meeting, they will be there, no matter what. You can also trust them to make sure that the practical decisions get made and that deadlines are met.

Your Own Personality Profile

Now that you have read about the various personality types along these four different dimensions, can you identify your own four characteristics? Are you an extrovert who makes logical decisions based on your five senses and who sticks to deadlines? Are you an introvert who operates on intuition, makes more emotionally based decisions, and likes to remain loose and flexible? Or are you some other combination of all of these characteristics?

If you can't readily identify your own particular type on each dimension based on my descriptions, you can take the self-scored test in Appendix B. (And you can find sources of additional information on it in Appendix A.) It is important for you to identify your own qualities—and the strengths and weaknesses that go along with them—in order for you to establish good working relationships with others.

It will also be important for all of your team members to identify their own personality profiles as a first step toward working with one another in the most cooperative manner possible. It would therefore be a good idea if you returned to this exercise once you have formed your problem-solving team later in this chapter so that each team member can do the exercise and share the results with the larger group.

Exercise 3.1: Personality Test

What is your own personality profile?

Extroverted or introverted?

Sensing or intuitive?

Thinking or feeling?

Judging or perceiving?

If you cannot identify your type, use the personality type assessment in Appendix B.

What is your personality profile based on that personality type assessment?

Seeing Others' Personality Strengths

Once you understand your own style, the next step is to identify the best ways and advantages of combining forces with individuals who are different from you. This is what the next exercise is about.

Before you immerse yourself in the exercise, let's spend some time with Julia, an extroverted, sensing, feeling, and judging individual who works as a sales manager. Julia's supervisor is Alex, the director of marketing. His personality profile is extroverted, intuitive, feeling, and perceptive. Julia and Alex share two personality dimensions, which gives their relationship some innate advantages. They are both extroverts, which got them off to a great start. They love to network and generate sales leads, and they enjoy doing it together. Moreover, they both consider the feelings of others when making serious decisions.

However, they differ on the other two personality dimensions. Julia prefers to use data and hard facts to solve problems, while Alex likes to use his intuition. Julia also likes to schedule time diligently and stick to deadlines, while Alex likes to keep things loose. Although this initially seemed like a problem to the two of them, after working together for a while they realized that these differences could work to their advantage in many ways. For example, when Julia is interested in brainstorming ideas for ways of selling new products, she turns to intuitive Alex, as he is naturally inclined to visualize approaches to doing things that have never been attempted before. And Alex loves to involve Julia when he is finalizing plans to launch products. She has a knack not only for creating efficient plans based on proven history and facts but also for following up on deadlines during implementation. Moreover, Julia has found Alex's perceiving dimension beneficial. It makes things easier for her when she wants to try new ideas, as he is flexible with decisions. In addition, he keeps a loose schedule and has an open-door policy. This means that Julia can easily meet with him.

Can you see how you, too, can use your personality differences with others to your advantage in working with them to solve problems?

Exercise 3.2: Seeing the Positives in Anyone

Think of an individual with whom you are working and who you consider to be "difficult." This is someone who sometimes pushes you to your limits.

1. Try to guess his or her personality type.
   - Does this person prefer to be with others or alone (extroversion versus introversion)?
   - Does this person prefer to base his or her understanding of the world on facts and using the five senses or on intuition (sensing versus intuiting)?
   - Does this person operate more from the head or the heart (thinking versus feeling)?
   - Does this person prefer efficiency or flexibility (judging versus perceiving)?

   List this person's four resulting personality characteristics.

2. Which of the four dimensions do both of you share, and on which do you differ?

3. What advantages can you see in working with this individual, based on your common personality dimensions?

4. What advantages can you see in working with this person, based on your dissimilar personality dimensions?

5. Now list three to five steps that you can implement when work-ing with this person in order to capitalize on the advantages that you now see.

Communicating Effectively

It is a well-accepted fact that relationships are built on three staples: trust, rapport, and respect. Creating and maintaining each of these qualities requires effective communication. Effective communica-tion is what takes you quickly through storming toward norming and performing in problem solving. It is what allows you to resolve conflict successfully and establish realistic expectations for all the parties involved.

Spinning Doughnuts into Gold

Years ago, a friend told me how his boss, Sherry, salvaged one of their training projects through effective communication. Sherry and her team set up a crucial meeting with a project monitor who was to determine whether they would receive funding for their pro-ject or not. At the meeting, one of the team members brought doughnuts to welcome the monitor. Much to the team's dismay, for nearly an hour the monitor focused the entire conversation on doughnuts, doughnut shops, and doughnut-making processes.

Everyone began looking for an excuse to leave the room or take a break—except Sherry. She stayed with the monitor, listening attentively and asking questions. She found out that the monitor's family had owned a doughnut shop, and she was eventually able to steer him into a discussion of how life had brought him to his current profession and—more importantly—what he was looking for in new programs such as theirs.

As a result of having attended carefully to what the monitor was communicating about his own personal style, needs, and goals, Sherry was able, during the last twenty minutes of the meeting, to present her team's program in terms she sensed the monitor would be able to understand and accept. Indeed, he quickly approved the program, with minor changes. Everyone was struck by the degree of trust that the monitor seemed to have in the team and the project, despite the fact that he had never worked with any of these people before.

This story has stayed with me over the years as a great example of how effective communication can be used to establish trust. Let's now look more specifically at the elements of effective communication.

Communicating Is About Listening

Authors Dale Carnegie and Stephen Covey have devoted a good deal of their influential work to this topic. Carnegie, in his classic *How to Win Friends and Influence People*, advises that if you want to become a good conversationalist, you should first become a good listener and encourage others to speak.

More recently, Covey, in *The Seven Habits of Highly Effective People*, emphasizes that excellence in communication is established by seeking first to understand and then to be understood. Henry Ford phrased it very nicely when he said, "If there is any secret to success, it lies in the ability to get the other person's point of view and see things from his angle as well as from your own."

In other words, effective communication is as much about active listening and asking the right questions as it is about responding to what is said and expressing what you think. *Active listening* requires establishing eye contact with the person who is speaking, paying attention to what the person is saying and how he or she is saying it, not interrupting, and not judging what is said.

By giving priority to the other person in conversation, you show that person respect. And this pays huge dividends in terms of building rapport and trust—crucial elements when you are working together in the problem-solving process. In addition, it provides you with information about who the person is—about his or her values, interests, and passions. As a result, when it comes time for you to communicate your own needs and desires, you will know how to express what you say in the other person's terms and often in his or her own language. This will go a long way toward helping you work with the other person to meet your own goals.

Again, that's precisely what Sherry did. She focused her attention on the project monitor, listened actively, and encouraged him to speak by asking questions. Thus she started to build trust, rapport, and respect right away. By listening actively, she was also able to gather the data she needed about what the monitor was looking for in a program that he would be willing to fund, and she was consequently able to tailor her presentation according to his criteria.

Conversely, active listening allows you to determine quickly whether the other person has any interest at all in what you hope to achieve. In problem solving, active listening will give you the data you need to find out fairly quickly whether you want to include this person in your problem-solving team or whether you want to move on—thus saving you time and effort in the long run. Moreover, active listening will provide you with the keys to working more effectively with individuals about whose inclusion on your team or whose interactions in your organization you have no choice. By giving you the opportunity to figure out what is important to others and what their personality style is, active listening will give you pointers as to how to communicate, support, inspire, and bring out the best in them. It will also help you accept them and refrain from trying to change them in any way. This alone can often help your group avoid the kinds of personality clashes that can bring problem solving to a halt.

Focusing on the other person's point of view is also the first step toward resolving conflicts effectively—a necessity during the storming phase. Once you understand the other person's position as well as your own, you can develop common goals, which serve as the basis of effective conflict resolution.

Similarly, understanding other people's viewpoints will help you and your team determine which ideas you have in common, and these will form the basis of your eventual solution. Moreover, as your team members continue to focus on understanding the strengths and weaknesses of different solution options, you will be able to enhance your solution by adding new ideas to it. This is how you can synthesize effective solutions for your problems (for more on this, see Chapter Seven).

Pointers for establishing effective communication are presented in Exhibit 3.1.

Exhibit 3.1 Guidelines for Effective Communication

- Make the other person the priority in conversation. When building a relationship with someone, let it be all about that person.

- Ask the other person questions in order to find out about his or her values and interests.

- Be genuinely interested in what the other person has to say.

- Listen fully without interrupting and judging.

- Pay attention to what is *not* being said. Look at the person's body language and facial expressions to gather additional information about what he or she is thinking and feeling.

Forming Your Problem-Solving Team

Now that you have a few more tools at your disposal for cultivating successful relationships with others, it is time to use them to put together the team you will need to solve the pressing challenge that you identified in Chapter One.

Most organizational problems call for solutions that affect others. They involve change. By embracing the individuals who will be affected by the solution and involving them in the problem-solving process, you win the battle against resistance to change. Still others may need to be involved because they are important decision makers or decision influencers or because they have key expertise. If you are the "owner" of the problem, you may already know most of these individuals. If you are not, you will need to partner with that "owner" in order to create a problem-solving team. This is exactly what I did with the president of the printing company mentioned earlier who needed to design a plant layout.

The next exercise helps you analyze your problem and identify the people with whom you need to work to devise and implement solutions.

Exercise 3.3: Identifying the Right Team Members

Think about the challenge you selected in Chapter One as your most important problem to solve.

Stage One

Working either by yourself or with the "owner" of the problem at hand, list the following:

1. Who might be affected by the solution to this particular issue?

2. Who will make the decisions related to this problem?

3. Who has influence over these decision makers?

4. Whose interests will be served by resolving this problem?

5. Who would be motivated to assist you in solving this problem?

Stage Two

The next set of questions relates to the skills and personality dimensions required to find solutions. Take your best stab at them without overanalyzing the situation.

1. Briefly, what are the most important core skills and expertise that solving your problem may require?

2. Who has these skills and expertise?

3. Which intuitive-type individuals can you involve during the first two steps, visioning and creating ideas?

4. Which sensing-type (fact-oriented) individuals can you involve during the third and fourth steps, developing the solution and taking action?

Communicating with Potential Team Members

You have now identified potential team members in the service of your problem. You may already have relationships with some of these individuals. But you will also need to communicate about the project with others you may not know as well. This is where you will employ the art of active listening.

I recommend that you set up individual meetings with each potential team member. First ask questions to find out what the person thinks about the problem and whether he or she is interested in being a part of the solution. Then ask questions to encourage the individual to speak more generally about his or her interests, needs, values, and motivations.

Having done some preliminary thinking about your problem and the kinds of resources that might be needed to solve it, this active listening process will give you a chance to see what strengths and capabilities each person will bring to the problem-solving process. It will also allow you to see things from each person's angle in addition to your own. You will thus be able to communicate about the problem and enlist the support of others using concepts and language with which they will readily be able to identify and in terms that will speak directly to their own values, desires, interests, and needs.

Suppose that you are working on a leadership development program for your company's managers. This program may include different components, such as training, peer support, or a new reward system. If, after talking with a potential team member, you discover that she is highly interested in peer support, be certain to let her know that she will have a chance to work on this component by getting involved.

The next exercise will guide you in this direction.

Exercise 3.4: Communicating with Potential Team Members

Set up a one-on-one meeting with each person you have identified as a potential team member. Ask the following questions in the order in which they are listed, being sure to listen actively to the other person's responses.

1. What do you think about the problem?

2. What do you need or want to see happen with this problem?

3. What are your motivations regarding the problem?

4. What is your professional background?

5. What are your personal interests?

6. What is your personality style? (You may need to explain the dimensions a little to help the person figure it out).

    Are you extroverted or introverted?

    Sensing or intuitive?

Thinking or feeling?

Judging or perceiving?

7. Are you interested in being a member of the problem-solving team?

8. What skills and abilities would you bring to the problem-solving process? How could those skills best be applied to that process?

Based on this person's personality profile and the replies to your questions, determine when his or her participation would be most beneficial (during the initial visioning and idea generation steps, during the later solution development and action steps, or both).

If by the end of the interview you feel that this person would make a good member of the problem-solving team, make your best attempt to establish his or her commitment to the new project. Try to put it in terms that this individual can identify with based on his or her needs, values, skills, interests, and personal style.

Setting Up the First Team Meeting

Invite to a first official meeting all the individuals you have identified as potential members of your core problem-solving team. Invite more people than you think you will need. Be sure to have all of the personality dimensions well represented. I recommend that you also invite players who you thought were strong candidates but who were not enthusiastic about the project. Recognize that some will eventually drop out, while others who seemed reluctant at first may become excited by the prospect of working on the team once they see the energy being generated around the project.

Although the first meeting starts the formation of the team, I generally find that it is not until the second or third meeting that the core team actually takes form. Also keep in mind that the team can expand and contract throughout the process. For example, certain key decision makers and key experts may choose not to participate actively until the third step of the problem-solving process, developing the solution. Moreover, you can invite other individuals to critical meetings. For example, you can involve additional intuitive types during the first two steps, visioning and creating ideas. And you can bring in sensing or judging types with budget and planning expertise during the last two steps, developing the solution and taking action.

Chapter Four will show you how to set the agenda for the first official meeting. It will also show you how to use the art of facilitation to make all of your subsequent teamwork as productive as possible.

Points to Remember

- Using teams is the best way to find solutions to complex problems.

- Relationships and teams go through four stages: forming, storming, norming, and performing. Storming is the most difficult stage.

- Moving your team from storming to performing is accomplished more quickly when team members build effective relationships.

- Understanding your own and others' personality characteristics is the first step in working well with others in problem solving.

- Communicating effectively is an important element in establishing trust, rapport, and respect.

- Effective communication is based on active listening, which you can use to help you put together your problem-solving team.

Chapter Four

Group Facilitation

Great discoveries and achievements invariably
involve the cooperation of many minds.
—*Alexander Graham Bell*

Now that you have selected your core team members, what's the
best way to work with them in order to engage in problem solving?

I learned something important about this back in my early
twenties, when I was hired to do work redesign for various func-
tional units at a major bank. For each unit, I interviewed all the
employees involved, asking them how they carried out their functions and what their suggestions were for improving their work
processes. I also observed them in action. Based on these data, I
came up with a detailed plan for work redesign, including new procedures and restructured roles for improved efficiency. I presented
my plan to the manager of a given unit and then moved on to the
next function.

I soon realized that my methods were producing neither a great
number of ideas nor the enthusiasm and commitment needed on
the part of the individuals involved for implementation. Most of
"my" proposed redesigns simply collected dust and left the managers dissatisfied.

This made me question not only my methods but also the way
in which I interacted with the stakeholders of each unit. I realized
that most of the ideas I was developing—and the knowledge about
the various functions—really rested with the employees of each

unit. All I was doing was verbalizing the suggestions they were generously offering, adding my own personal synthesis and insight.

That's when the idea hit me: Why don't I involve these employees in designing their own solutions? I drastically changed my methods. I started with a few interviews and observations to gain insight into the situation but quickly moved into holding a facilitated meeting with all of the employees who would be affected by the changes. During the meeting, I assumed the role of listener rather than expert. I supported the group's members in verbalizing and synthesizing their ideas for a new work process. Most of "our" solutions did get implemented.

I had inadvertently stumbled upon the magic of facilitation, the glue that makes it all stick. And I never looked back.

Facilitation gives teams the tools they need to organize themselves, confront their issues, and move quickly into the norming and performing stages. In fact, Michael Doyle and David Straus, authors of *How to Make Meetings Work*, observe that some organizations find that they can increase productivity by 15 percent through facilitation.

What You Will Learn in This Chapter

This chapter will provide you with the tools you need to facilitate your problem-solving team effectively. The process includes the following activities:

- Understanding the elements of facilitation and the role of the facilitator
- Learning how to brainstorm and prioritize
- Learning how to run meetings effectively

Bear in mind that this chapter will concentrate on the basics of group facilitation only. This is a vast topic, however. If you wish to learn more about it, consult the resources listed in Appendix A at the back of the book.

What Is Facilitation?

If you want to work with your team to solve problems in the most effective way possible, you must learn the art of facilitation. Facilitation encompasses a set of tools for structuring and conducting group meetings that allow for maximum participation of all individuals present. In facilitated meetings, the facilitator serves as a guide who enables team members to share their views, brainstorm and prioritize ideas, and synthesize them into solutions.

The role of the facilitator is different from the role of the leader. Leaders are the owners of the meeting. They participate in discussions, influence views, and make decisions. They also direct the traffic of the group—that is, the way participants interact and the methods by which decisions are made in order to move the meeting forward.

Facilitators direct the traffic of the group as well, but they remain neutral on what is being discussed. They focus on group process, on *how* each item is discussed. Their duties are to regulate participation and assist the team members in establishing objectives, generating ideas, and meeting team goals. They free up leaders to do what they do best: participate, influence, and make decisions. Because the facilitator's neutrality is a key function of the role, it is important that the facilitator of a particular meeting be someone whose day-to-day work will not be affected by the team's decisions.

Four facilitator functions are of the greatest importance:

1. Asking questions to stimulate participation and clarify meaning

2. Listening actively

3. Keeping the meeting emotionally safe

4. Recording meeting content effectively

Asking Questions

Facilitators *elicit participation* from group members and help them clarify their ideas, primarily by asking questions. For example, to get the creative juices of team members flowing, facilitators may ask open-ended questions such as these:

> "How would you approach this issue if you had all the resources you needed?"

> "Let's shoot for the stars! What would you do if you had a magic wand?"

> "Assuming ideal circumstances, what would you do to turn the situation around?"

Other questions seek to *clarify the meaning* of participants' statements and views:

> "So you are saying that . . . Is this correct?"

> "Tell us more about your view. What do you mean by . . . ?"

Closed-ended questions aim to summarize or conclude a discussion so that the meeting can either move on to another topic or come to an end. Such questions are framed like these:

> "Do you all agree with this idea?"

> "So can we also include X in the solution?"

> "Is this acceptable?"

Listening Actively

Facilitation involves 80 percent listening and only 20 percent speaking. There are several techniques that facilitators can employ to listen actively and effectively, including the following:

- Face the speaker.
- Make eye contact with the speaker.

- Show genuine interest in the speaker and what he or she is saying, but refrain from judging what is said.
- When appropriate, move actively about the room as a means of energizing team members to continue to participate.

Keeping the Meeting Safe

Facilitators regulate the order and manner in which participants interact, thereby enabling team members to share their views in a safe, nonjudgmental forum. This promotes not only maximum creativity but also clarity regarding the various viewpoints being expressed—both of which are essential for decision making. The facilitator provides the structure so that meeting participants do all of the following:

- Speak when their turn comes rather than interrupting each other
- Share their views regardless of their position in the company
- Stay focused on the meeting agenda
- Resolve conflicts effectively by concentrating on achieving a desired outcome rather than negotiating personal differences
- Explain their views so that all participants understand
- Start and end the meetings on time

Exhibit 4.1 provides a number of suggestions for keeping the meeting safe in different situations.

Recording Meeting Content

Facilitators help the team members visually keep tabs on the content of their discussions by recording it on flipcharts or other media. Their purpose is to make the content of the meeting as visible as possible while keeping the process almost invisible. The art of recording and

Exhibit 4.1 Keeping the Meeting Safe

Situation	Suggestion
One person dominates the discussion.	"Thank you for your valuable idea. What do others think?"
Some individuals are quiet and do not participate.	"Can we hear from all of you who have not participated yet?" Or the facilitator can break the group into small teams and ask that all teams take turns providing input.
There are side discussions among participants that distract from the process.	Refer to established ground rules or create new ones. Or say: "Perhaps we are failing to capture some great ideas. Can you share your thoughts with us?"
Someone becomes emotional about an issue.	"You seem to feel strongly about this. Can you help the team understand why you feel this way?"
Someone keeps repeating a specific point.	Perhaps the participant feels that he or she is not well understood. The facilitator can say: "This is an important issue. Let's discuss it in more detail and come to an agreement so that we will not have to cover it again. What do others think?" Discussion items are recorded. If the participant repeats it again, say: "I believe that we covered that item in detail. Unless there is something new, I think that we can move to the next item . . ."
There is conflict between two participants.	"What do others think about this?" If the conflict continues: "It seems that you are both concentrating on what you don't have in common. Can you identify what you both desire in this situation?"

exhibiting information effectively could take up a whole book in itself. Here, however, are a few guidelines facilitators adhere to:

- Listen carefully, clarify what has been said, and then write it down exactly—not your interpretation of it.
- Print or use block letters.
- Use blue or another dark color for most of the recording and red or orange to highlight important points.
- Make sure everyone in the room can understand what you have written.
- Use diagrams such as flowcharts to describe processes, as appropriate.
- Be consistent.
- Number each consecutive flipchart page.

Guidelines for Effective Meetings

Using an outside facilitator enhances group interaction and will move your team into the norming and performing stages much faster. If you can't afford to hire a professional facilitator, you can still make your meetings more effective by appointing an *internal* facilitator. Ideally, this person should be someone who has been trained to run meetings. As noted earlier, he or she should be someone whose daily duties will not be affected by the outcome of the meeting. This makes it easier for the person to remain neutral about the content of the meeting.

What follows are some guidelines that can help you, your internal facilitator, and your problem-solving team hold the most productive meetings possible.

Preparing for the Meeting

Effective meetings begin with and depend on excellent preparation. This includes setting the agenda, compiling all required materials, and selecting and preparing the meeting space.

The agenda, a written document that sets forth the objective(s) of the meeting and the items for discussion, is drawn up by the facilitator in partnership with the project owner and all team participants. The facilitator can assemble agenda items by talking with team members and other key participants. Or he or she might write up a sample agenda with the project owner and then finalize it by talking with team members and other key participants. Beside each agenda item is listed a realistic time estimate for its completion and a brief description of how it will be discussed (see Exhibit 4.2). Keep in mind that no agenda is absolutely final until the meeting actually begins. Should participants voice valid concerns or brilliant ideas for changes prior to that, effective facilitators support them by modifying the agenda appropriately.

In addition, the facilitator works with the project sponsor to select a meeting place that maximizes group interaction. You might, for example, want to choose a room with a large oval table or one in which the chairs can be rearranged into a semicircle.

Starting the Meeting Right

There are two extremely important items that must be established at the beginning of any meeting: ground rules and criteria for meeting success. Together, these items create the appropriate code of behavior and expectations for the group.

Ground rules are a set of expected behaviors of meeting order and interaction. The facilitator helps the team develop and agree on these parameters, and records and keeps them displayed at the front of the room. He or she starts by explaining the concept of ground rules, provides a couple of examples that everyone can understand and relate to, and invites the team members to provide additional suggestions. Here are some examples:

- Everyone is expected to participate.
- All ideas are welcome.
- We must start and end the meeting on time.

- We do not interrupt the speaker.
- Side discussions among participants are not permitted.
- We all come to the meeting prepared.
- We stick to items on the agenda and set up other meetings to discuss related topics.

The facilitator reminds the group of these parameters at the start of meetings, particularly those held during the team's forming and storming stages. He or she also takes the initiative to enforce these parameters during these phases. Should the team members disregard one or more ground rules, the facilitator intervenes by stating: "I believe we need to pause here. I am noticing that our norms are being broken. Let's spend some time discussing our ground rules. What is happening? What do we need to change?" As the group progresses toward norming and performing, the participants naturally take the lead to maintain these rules.

The facilitator also helps the group establish criteria for meeting success. These are statements of intent for the gathering and other indicators that the meeting has gone successfully. Examples of success criteria are "We will resolve all budget issues in this meeting" or "We will generate at least thirty ideas for resolving this problem." The facilitator also records these on the flipchart. He or she can help monitor meeting progress by periodically asking participants to gauge their performance against the criteria for meeting success. At the end of the meeting, participants can have a concluding discussion to see how well they have done against these criteria.

Running the Meeting

If you use an internal facilitator and not a professional one from the outside, you may want to consider dividing up some of the facilitator's tasks among several people. Specifically, you may want to assign a recorder, a timekeeper, and a minute taker. Doing so is particularly helpful when meetings have more than fifteen participants, as it allows the facilitator to focus on the dynamics and the

Exhibit 4.2 Sample Agenda

Meeting Objective: To create a vision statement for the problem

Agenda Item	Process
1. Welcome and overview (20 minutes)	The participants review the meeting objective and the agenda items with the help of the facilitator.
	The facilitator provides an overview of the concept of a vision statement.
2. Review of ground rules (10 minutes)	The participants review effective behaviors of participation and interaction with the support of the facilitator.
3. Establishment of criteria for meeting success (10 minutes)	The participants decide on success standards for the meeting.
4. Discussion of the problem (30 minutes)	The facilitator guides the team in discussing what needs to change about the present situation and all areas where improvement is needed.
5. Generation of ideas (90 minutes)	The facilitator introduces the concept of brainstorming and guides participants to suggest as many ideas as possible.
	Participants offer ideas for their vision statement, the ideal picture of a successful resolution.
	The facilitator records all idea suggestions on charts.

6. Break (10 minutes)

7. Selection of key phrases (20 minutes)

The facilitator guides participants to underline all the words, phrases, and sentences that they feel are meaningful for inclusion in the vision statement. The facilitator records these key phrases.

The facilitator helps the participants prioritize and select the most important key phrases. The facilitator also makes a record of these determinations.

8. Drafting of the vision statement (45 minutes)

The participants use the prioritized phrases to synthesize a draft vision statement. The facilitator records the statement and guides the participants in refining it.

9. Discussion of next steps (15 minutes)

The participants discuss the next steps for finalizing the vision statement, evaluate the session against success criteria, and set a time and date for the next meeting.

10. Adjournment

traffic of the interaction and frees him or her from getting bogged down in writing on the flipcharts.

The recorder thus assumes the role of scribing the content of the discussions on the flipchart. The timekeeper maintains an eye on the clock, notifies the group when time limits are being approached or have been reached, and reminds the group to get back on track when time guidelines are broken. The minute taker prepares notes from the meeting as soon as it has concluded and distributes them to all participants.

Some additional activities the facilitator can engage in include the following:

- Helping group members follow the ground rules and suggesting when it may be necessary for them to add more rules
- Using the techniques of brainstorming and prioritizing, where appropriate (see Exhibit 4.3)
- Supporting the group in using a variety of creativity techniques (see Chapter Six)
- Encouraging disagreement based on facts rather than personalities, as this is the source of innovation (see Chapter Seven for more directions on how to achieve this)
- Leading the team to make decisions by consensus rather than by voting (this point will be discussed further in Chapter Seven)
- Monitoring meeting progress by periodically asking participants to gauge their performance against the criteria for meeting success.

Closing the Meeting

At the end of the meeting, the facilitator helps the group define the steps that must take place prior to the next gathering. He or she also leads participants in evaluating the meeting by discussing what they feel went well, what needs to be improved, and how improvements

Exhibit 4.3 Two Indispensable Facilitation Tools

Brainstorming

Brainstorming—the process of throwing out ideas in unedited fashion—is one of the most effective ways of generating solution ideas. The facilitator is responsible for conducting the brainstorming process in meetings in which this activity is deemed appropriate by guiding the group to do the following:

- Define the objective of the brainstorming session (see Chapter Six for examples)
- Generate as many ideas as possible
- Encourage participation from all members
- Discourage censure and judgments of ideas
- Expand on previously mentioned items
- Refrain from discussing the ideas at this stage

Prioritizing

After the brainstorming process is concluded, ideas can be honed down through prioritizing. For this, the facilitator guides the team to do the following:

- Highlight the ideas they deem most important (usually two to five ideas)
- Vote in round-robin fashion on each of the ideas and record the tallies next to each item
- Count the scores and write down the ideas with the highest scores on another chart

should be made. Finally, the facilitator summarizes the next steps for the group and thanks the participants.

You're now ready to go to work on addressing your key problem. These initial four chapters have provided you with the cornerstones for building your solution. The next chapter will take you through the first step of the process: crafting your ideal vision of the perfect solution.

Points to Remember

- Facilitation helps you move your team into the performing stage more quickly.

- Facilitation is a method of structuring and conducting group meetings that allows for maximum participation of all individuals present.

- Facilitators serve as guides who enable team members to effectively share their views, brainstorm and prioritize ideas, and synthesize them into solutions.

- Even when you cannot afford the services of a professional facilitator, you can still achieve performance excellence by appointing an internal facilitator.

- Effective meetings require a good deal of preparation.

- Starting your meetings right involves setting ground rules and establishing criteria for success.

Chapter Five

Starting with a Clear Vision

Vision is the art of seeing the invisible.

—Jonathan Swift

Years ago, I helped introduce Western management tools to a group of business leaders from one of the former socialist republics. One of the first topics we covered was how to turn current challenges into opportunities. Naturally, we talked about the concept of creating a "vision" for the solution—the ideal outcome that we desire for our challenges over the next five or ten years.

We talked about the magic that vision statements generate to help organizations become more innovative and focused on excellence, and we discussed all of the steps necessary to formulate such a statement. I then asked the members of the group to put together a vision statement for one of their own challenges.

I was astonished to find that some of them had difficulty with both the concept of "vision" and the exercise. In fact, they did not even attempt it. Their response was, "We cannot put together an idealistic statement like this. Our employees would not take this seriously because it is unrealistic."

Although this experience was particularly striking because of the cultural attitudes of these business leaders, I have also seen this kind of resistance operating in more subtle ways in companies in the United States. Often people hold the belief that problem-solving ideas need to be "realistic" in order to be effective. But while realistic thinking has its merits, ultimately it can be limiting. Realistic thinking is not going to help you to break new ground and create new opportunities. If you want to solve problems effectively and do great things, you have to think out of the box. You have to move out of the stale, immobile picture of things as they are into the world of new possibilities. It is this kind of breakthrough thinking that has led, as a matter of fact, to some of the world's greatest inventions, including the airplane, the personal computer, and the cellular phone. Walt Disney, who established one of the world's most innovative corporations, encapsulated his success in four words: "Think, believe, dream, and dare."

What You Will Learn in This Chapter

The first step in working with your team to solve problems is to create a clear and bold vision for the ideal outcome of your problem. The vision statement need not go into the specifics of how the problem will be solved. Rather, it is a broad inspirational statement that serves as a beacon for developing ideas and alternatives, selecting the best solution, and putting together an action plan regarding a given problem.

This chapter will help you more fully understand the components and the importance of the visioning process in problem solving. It will also take you and your team through a series of exercises, a step-by-step process to think deeply about your desires, dreams, passions, skills, and talents as they relate to your organization and your challenge. You will then work together to synthesize your vision. The end result will be a statement that will become your motivator and guide for arriving at an innovative solution to the problem that you identified in Chapter One.

Clear Vision for Glass Deco

The following case offers an excellent example of how a company used visioning to start their problem-solving process.

Mike was the new vice president of business development at Glass Deco, a manufacturer of decorative glass pieces that had been founded in the early 1900s. Mike's first assignment was to work with the company's ten top executives to create a new marketing image for the firm.

After the first three meetings with the executives, a problem became apparent: the executives did not know how to operate as a team. The meetings were turning into gripe sessions about how things at the company were not working, how everyone's expectations were not being met, and how different departments were not pulling in the same direction. Each executive seemed to be focusing on the goals of his or her department rather than the goals of the company as a whole.

It was clear to Mike that the first step in addressing the problem of the group's fragmentation was to have the executives create a vision for their problem of how to work together effectively as a unified team. With the support of the company CEO, Mike planned a two-day retreat at a local hotel for the executives and hired an outside facilitator to support the process.

The first day began with a series of structured events that allowed the participants to vent their complaints. After a couple of hours, as the venting started to dissipate, the vice president of product design suddenly said, "OK, so now we know what happened in the past. We know what doesn't work. But we all want the same thing: a strong and profitable company that produces the most beautiful and innovative glass products. How can we work together to achieve this? What would our team look like if we had no barriers?"

That was it! The magic started to happen. The executives began talking about everything that was positive about the situation. Their enthusiasm and can-do attitude emerged. They spent the rest of the day defining the ideal way in which they could function as a team. They shared what they desired for their team and visualized how things would work smoothly if they all adopted the company's goals as their own. They further talked about how their individual passions and dreams could be incorporated into their work together. Finally, they reviewed all the skills and talents that they already had and could call on to make the shift to operating as a cross-functional unit.

The executives spent the second day synthesizing their ideas into a vision statement for their team. They then refined their thoughts and generated ideas about how to make their vision happen. By the end of the day, they had decided to focus on establishing clear mechanisms and procedures for cooperation, communication, and problem solving across departments. They also agreed that human resources would work on aligning the company's reward and recognition system with both departmental and organizational goals.

Mike and his CEO had orchestrated a small revolution. By focusing on the possibilities, the executive team members became filled with enthusiasm and optimism about the future. As they did so, they moved away from finger-pointing and toward agreement and commitment for taking action. They were able to work as a team to create a new image for Glass Deco. The result was a dramatic improvement in both client satisfaction and profitability.

Exhibit 5.1 presents the Glass Deco vision statement that the executive team put together. Note that it is stated in the present tense, as if it is happening already. Moreover, you'll notice that it not only addresses the immediate problem—of being unable to work together as a team—but also goes beyond it. It paves the way for further opportunities for the executive team in the long run. You will also observe that some items of this statement relate to the vision of the company as a whole. This is because of the nature of the challenge, which is located at the top of Glass Deco's organizational hierarchy, with the leadership team. Many of your problems will not reside at the top of your company's hierarchy and will not be linked directly to your company vision. Yet as you go through the exercises in this chapter, keep in mind that you, too, will be crafting your own vision statement for your problem, one that goes beyond just your immediate challenge.

Exhibit 5.1 Glass Deco Executive Team Vision Statement

- We work as a team to create the most innovative, most beautiful, and highest-quality glass products in the industry.

- We work collaboratively to achieve Glass Deco's goals for profitability, revenue, and customer satisfaction.

- We cooperate, communicate, and solve problems across functions.

- We are recognized and rewarded for our work in meeting the company's goals as well as the goals of our own departments.

The Visioning Process

Before we examine the visioning process, let's get a clearer idea of exactly what a vision statement is.

The Vision Statement

A vision statement can be defined as the ideal outcome that you desire for your challenge over the next five to ten years. It is not a statement of the solution to the problem, nor does it provide the specific ideas, tactics, or details involved in developing and implementing the solution. Instead, the vision statement paints the ideal picture of what you want to accomplish. Think of it as your ultimate destination, devoid of the specific details on how to get there. The details are what you will spend the next three chapters putting together. The vision statement, the focus of this chapter, is a simple and concise, yet heartfelt and enthusiastic, statement that incorporates answers to some or all of the following questions:

- What do you most desire for your situation?
- What would your situation look like if there were no barriers and you could shoot for the stars?

- What would the solution to your challenge look like if it included your dreams?

- What would you change if you had a magic wand?

- What would you do if you had all the resources in the world?

- How could you capitalize on your skills and talents to help turn the present situation around?

- What would your situation be if you could capitalize on your passions?

The vision statement serves as the beacon for the problem-solving process and an inspirational guide for you, your team, and your organization. It is intended to become a "self-fulfilling prophecy"—an intention that you plan to see brought to fruition.

The vision outlined in your statement represents a place where you and your team have never been before. The trip you take to get there will require you to maximize your creativity and imagination. It will call on you to use your right brain, the part of the mind that operates on intuition, your sixth sense. This is the part of you that does not need to come up with numbers to support your ideas. It's the part that simply knows when things "feel right."

How the Visioning Process Works

The visioning process provides you and your team with an opportunity to think deeply about what it is you desire—something that Peter Senge, in *The Fifth Discipline*, stresses is an important element that is often lacking in the workplace. Your exploration will also include your dreams and passions. Moreover, it will bring into the mix your team's skills and talents (see Figure 5.1).

Developing a vision statement in this way is a powerful activity, for several reasons. First, it fills both you and your team with the necessary energy, enthusiasm, and optimism for creating and implementing solutions. It takes you into the world of *possibilities* beyond your current challenge.

Figure 5.1 The Visioning Process

Second, by allowing you to consider your desires, dreams, and passions for your challenge, the visioning process helps you and your team members develop a deeper sense of meaning about your work. It thereby generates a powerful psychological contract among you, which becomes the basis for a deep *commitment* to the work and to your organization. This, of course, is extremely important for the successful implementation of any solution.

Third, visioning is powerful because the final statement can function as the light at the end of the tunnel when things become difficult. It serves as a constant reminder of your most important *priorities*. In fact, when the going gets rough, spending some time with your vision statement can help you and your team refocus your thinking and stay on track.

Finally, the visioning process is extremely valuable because it allows you to focus on the solution rather than on the problem. Focusing on the problem involves you in wasting time assigning blame and going over everything that is wrong. You end up procrastinating and prolonging the problem. Visioning, by contrast, does not require you to analyze why things are the way they are. It helps you think about how you would like things to be. It also helps your team come to *agreement* about taking action. Isn't it easier to agree on what is possible than on who is to blame? That agreement serves as the glue that will hold your team together all the way through implementation.

Exercises for Creating Your Vision

I will now lead you through a series of exercises that will allow you to think about your desires for the opportunity you identified in Chapter One, including your dreams; discover or revisit your passions; consider how your skills and talents can come into play in creating a solution; and use the right-brain activity of visualization to generate ideas.

I recommend that you and each of your team members complete these exercises on your own. Think of completing them as embarking on your own kind of mini "retreat." Their purpose is to prepare all of you for the final step, during which you will craft your vision statement collectively.

You may want to be sure you have some intuitive individuals on your team, as they naturally prefer right-brain thinking. This is not an absolute requirement, however. All individuals are creative. Just remember to allow your ideas to surface and accept them at face value without questioning or judgment. Most important of all, have fun with this process! The more fun you have, the better your vision will be.

Your Desires and Dreams

The first exercise will help you explore what you and your team members truly desire regarding the solution to your challenge. Some of your desires may be related to what your customers need and want or what your competitors are doing. But I urge you to think far beyond customers and competition. For example, you may be working on a redesign project to simplify the components of a product to cut down on its cost. Yet your team members' desire may be to add some new features to it as well.

Some of your deepest desires relate to your dreams. Dreams are our deepest aspirations, hopes, and ambitions. Steve Jobs, of Apple, for instance, has a deep aspiration, an ambition, to create products that revolutionize the computer industry. As a result, he has been instrumental in the development of the Macintosh and more recently in reinventing the image of Apple as a company. Walt Disney similarly believed in the power of dreams. One of his famous quotes, in fact, can serve as your group motto: "If you can dream it, you can do it!"

You'll find that this exercise will create a powerful shift for you and many of your team members. This is partly because people are hardly ever asked about what they deeply desire. The opportunity to think about this issue will stimulate a great deal of energy. It will free everyone up to become a source of creativity. More importantly, it will result in the generation of not just lots of ideas—but lots of *creative* ideas.

Exercise 5.1: Your Desires and Dreams

What kind of an outcome do you want for your problem based on what you know about your customers' needs and wants?

What do you want accomplish in order to surpass your competition?

What do you *ideally desire* for the outcome of this problem, apart from how it relates to your customers and competitors?

What are your deepest desires, your dreams, about your work?

What would the resolution to your problem look like if it allowed for some of your dreams to come true? (For example, in a redesign project, if one of your real desires were to add features to the product, your deepest desire might be to redesign it completely and make it the best on the market.)

What result would you ask for if you had a magic wand?

Your Passions

The next factor to consider when developing your vision is how your passions can be brought into your work environment and be made a part of the ultimate solution to your problem. If *passion* is, as the dictionaries tell us, a form of boundless enthusiasm, *passions* are the objects of such boundless enthusiasm. In other words, passions are the interests, activities, and hobbies that fill us with fervor and excitement. Some passions may be related to the product of your organization. Many of the Glass Deco employees, for example, were passionate about the company's products. Or you might be working at a software company because of your passion for designing computer games. Other passions may be related to your function no matter what the product or service of the organization that employs you. Some individuals are in the sales profession because they thrive on making deals; others are filled with enthusiasm when assisting clients and work in customer service.

Numerous studies, authors, and business leaders point out that incorporating passions in the workplace brings the best out in people and holds the keys to the kind of creativity and adaptability that are needed in today's business world. According to Richard Chang,

CEO of Richard Chang & Associates, for example, harnessing employees' passion can provide the "single most powerful competitive advantage" for building organizational success. And Tom Kelley, general manager of IDEO, one of the world's most innovative design companies, states that passion is a crucial component of creativity and excellence in teams.

Exercise 5.2 is all about imagining what would happen if you were able to include your passions in your work life. It will allow you to reflect on what would happen to your organizational problem, in particular, if the resolution meant that you would be able to have some of those passions fulfilled. It is designed to fuel the excitement, inspiration, and creativity you will need for crafting a high-level vision statement. Again, you and each of your team members should complete this exercise independently.

Exercise 5.2: Your Passions

Think about all of the personal interests, hobbies, and activities that may have brought you to your present job. Which passions make you extremely enthusiastic about your current workplace?

What would the resolution of your current problem look like if it allowed for your passions to be expressed more fully? (For example, if you are a systems analyst for a consulting firm and have a passion for public speaking, including this passion in a project for creating new marketing strategies might not only lead to the generation of new sales leads for your firm but would also energize you personally.)

Your Skills and Talents

We all have skills and talents that we can draw on to take advantage of new opportunities. *Skills* are abilities and proficiencies that we have developed through our activities at work, at home, or with volunteer organizations. Some of these skills might include writing, speaking, planning and organizing events, negotiating, bookkeeping and accounting, drafting, painting, singing, writing music, or computer programming. Some of these skills we call talents. *Talents* are skills that seem particularly innate to us and that are often relatively effortless to develop.

The more you use your skills and talents, the better you become at them, and the easier it is to work with them. Other skills and talents may be dormant, just waiting to be unleashed.

The next exercise guides you to think about how your current skills and talents may find further expression in the ideal solution to your problem. It also lets you consider how skills and talents that you dream of developing or using in the future may be given a chance to emerge. The exercise will fill you with a can-do attitude and will help take you another step closer to creating your ideal vision for the problem at hand.

Exercise 5.3: Your Skills and Talents

What do you love to do?

What are you really good at?

What are some activities that you can do easily and effortlessly?

What are some other skills and talents that you would like to develop further if you could?

What would a solution to your problem look like if it allowed you to use more of your current skills and talents or to develop new ones? (Suppose that you are working on creating new marketing strategies for a product or service and are good at programming on the Web. Creating an electronic avenue for marketing would allow you to use and cultivate your skills and talents while at the same time further the company's objectives.)

Visualization: Using Your Right Brain for Breakthrough Ideas

As you begin to elaborate your vision, you may find that you want to put your imagination to even greater use. The business world has taught us to rely primarily on our left brain, with its logical, sequential, and measurement emphasis. Yet when you seek to maximize creativity, you cannot afford to resort to using your left brain only. You need to capitalize on your right brain, which is more intuitive and creative.

If you excelled in school and later in business, you may find that tapping into your right brain is almost a foreign experience. You have relied heavily on the left side of your brain, on facts and logical thinking, and this has carried you forward successfully for many years. You have probably put your right brain behind you, and you may even have minimized and discounted the times you have used it effectively. You may have had experiences, for example, in which you worked off "hunches"—a strongly right-brain activity—but you may have ultimately attributed your decisions and actions to your rational adherence to facts and data.

So it's time to dust off your right brain! You can use it to lead you to a vision statement for your problem that truly opens up new possibilities.

An activity called visualization can be extremely effective in helping you to tap into your right brain. *Visualization* is the process of creating imaginative mental pictures—in this case, of ideal outcomes for the problem at hand. It is something you can do on your own through relaxation, meditation, or self-hypnosis. Or you can do it by having someone verbally guide you. Guided visualization is one of the most effective ways for achieving breakthroughs.

In *guided visualization*, you close your eyes and allow yourself to relax by listening to a voice (either live or on tape) that leads you through a series of steps and instructions. Guided visualization can help you get in touch with your inner creativity and bring to light some very interesting insights regarding your problem. At the very least, it will give you a feeling of relaxation and even euphoria.

Many books on guided visualization are available. Reading them can enhance your understanding of and appreciation for this activity. I would recommend, however, that you give visualization a try by using a tape that you can probably find at your local bookstore. Appendix A lists the titles of some resources that you might find useful.

The following exercise guides you to visualize the ideal picture for your challenge. The best place for doing so depends on personal preference. For example, you may want to do the exercise sitting in a comfortable chair in a quiet room. You might also want to consider doing it by the ocean or a lake or in the woods.

Exercise 5.4: Visualization on Your Own

As a first step, close your eyes and calm your mind and body through relaxation or meditation. As you quiet your mind and feel more relaxed, you can simply visualize yourself discovering the ideal outcome for your challenge. Imagine yourself already there and experiencing the reality of it. You may see, hear, or just feel various messages that will give you new insights into your situation. You may also get messages from other people as you visualize them providing you with assistance.

What do you see?

What do you hear?

How do you feel?

What messages are you getting?

What are others doing?

What ideas are you receiving?

It may feel as though you are creating your own internal movie. Once you feel that you want to move on, you can open your eyes and reflect on the ideas you had about your problem and any possible directions for your vision statement.

Now write your insights down here or in a notebook.

You will be astonished at how many new ideas come to you during visualization if you stay open to the possibilities. And the more you can engage in the practice, the more comfortable you will become at "centering" yourself and "feeling" the opportunities.

Putting Your Vision Statement Together

To recap, your vision is the ideal outcome that you desire for your challenge over the next five or ten years. You now have specific ideas about what you truly desire to see happen with this problem, and you have considered how your desires, dreams, passions, skills, and talents can be involved in the solution. You have also come up with new ideas through visualization.

You're probably looking at all the wonderful ideas you have created and are wondering how to synthesize them into a vision statement without losing any of the ingredients. The next exercise will help you do just that. In fact, with the support of facilitation, you and your team members will be able to experience the *sigma effect*. You will be able not only to generate a lot more ideas as a team but also to interact and synthesize those ideas in ways that may surprise you. It is important that you and your team go through the following exercises with the assistance of an external or an internal facilitator.

The exercise is designed to be used with a small group of up to seven individuals. If you are working with more than seven people, see the next section, "Guidelines for Working with a Large Team," to modify the exercise. (Without such modification in a large group, the exercise could become unwieldy.)

Regard your vision statement as a work in progress. As your situation evolves, so will your vision. Yet after you have developed, reflected on, and refined your vision statement and you and your team members feel good about it, you can consider it "good enough" and move forward with the next steps of the problem-solving process. Look back at Exhibit 5.1 and then at the example in Exhibit 5.2 to become more familiar with what a vision statement reads like. The statement in Exhibit 5.2 presents the vision that was developed by the customer service department of a manufacturing organization.

Exhibit 5.2 Customer Service Vision Statement

- We provide exceptional customer service to both internal and external customers.

- We are trained and empowered to communicate effectively with our customers and continuously solve their problems.

- We are rewarded for achieving superior customer satisfaction.

- Our computer systems are built to support excellent customer service.

Exercise 5.5: Creating Your Vision Statement

Steps 1 and 2 are optional. Their purpose is to get to you and your team prepared to shed the inertia of the old and start to visualize your new reality along the lines of what was discussed in Chapter Two, "Positive Thinking: From Fear to Action."

Step 1. Reflecting on the Problem

As a group, think again about your problem. With the support of your facilitator, brainstorm together about what you would like to change and improve about this situation, and make a list of those items.

Step 2. Revisiting Your Positive Inventory

Each team member first revisits the positive inventory that he or she created in Chapter Two. Then have a facilitated discussion on everything that is positive for your group: situations, people, each individual's skills and talents, lessons, and experience.

Step 3. Brainstorming Ideas

This step consists of a brainstorming session with the objective of generating the maximum number of ideas for the ideal outcome that you desire for your challenge over the next five or ten years. The main question to ask is "What do we want to accomplish *ideally?*" (Remember, you are not looking to settle on specific action steps or projects yet; you are looking for ideas regarding what you would like the *final outcome* to look like.) At this stage, team members can offer the ideas they generated in the other exercises in this chapter, as well as additional ideas that will naturally come to them through effective brainstorming. Moreover, your facilitator could support you in creating additional ideas through visualization. Appendix C provides a team visualization exercise that you can use if you so choose.

Step 4. Underlining Key Phrases

At this point, team members review their ideas from step 3 as well as the group's positive inventory. Team members scan these materials and underline all the words, phrases, and sentences that stand out as the most significant and meaningful to them and that they consider to be important for inclusion in the vision statement.

Step 5. Listing Key Phrases

Group members share their key phrases while the facilitator records them on flipchart paper.

Step 6. Prioritizing Key Phrases

The group uses the prioritization technique outlined in Chapter Four to select the most important key phrases. The facilitator (or recorder) rewrites the most important key phrases on new flipchart pages.

Step 7. Drafting the Vision Statement

Group members use the words and sentences from step 5 to synthesize a sample vision statement. Remember to have fun with this process! This is only a draft.

Step 8. Refining the Vision Statement

Display and reflect on the statement that you have developed. Take the time to make any additions, corrections, or other needed changes. Make sure that the statement is simple, concise, and understandable to everyone. Keep refining it until everyone understands it and feels it is both optimal and suitable.

Guidelines for Working with a Large Team

Working with a large team—a group of more than twelve to fourteen individuals—to develop a vision statement can be a powerful and rewarding experience. Should you be working with a group of this size, the first thing to consider is where the visioning meeting should be held.

Depending on the complexity and size of your problem, its importance to your organization, and your available budget, you may wish to make the visioning process a special event by choosing a nice location for it. It has been demonstrated that off-site retreats spur participants' creativity and lead to more effective results. If your budget permits it, I would recommend that you choose a location with a lovely natural setting, such as a beautiful mountaintop, a lake, or a beach. An off-site locale is not a requirement, however. I have helped groups craft a vision statement right in their own workplace with excellent results.

You will want to be sure to define the agenda for your meetings. You can use the techniques of facilitation, discussed in Chapter Four, to maximize the team's time. As we discussed, this means that you will want to have an internal or external facilitator, and you will need to summarize group discussions on flipchart paper. In addition, you may use the technique of brainstorming to complete the first three steps of Exercise 5.5 and the activity of prioritizing to complete step 6. Again, you may want to review Chapter Four about brainstorming and prioritization.

To modify Exercise 5.5 appropriately for your group, you will need to consider time and its relationship to team size. A good rule of thumb is to have no more than seven individuals synthesizing a draft statement as a subgroup. With a group of seven to fourteen members, you could have two or even three subgroups and could complete your vision statement in four to eight hours (see the sample agenda in Exhibit 4.2). With a group larger than fourteen members, you will need additional time both for generating ideas and for synthesizing vision statements with multiple subgroups. It is best if you can take a couple of days to complete this process. If that is not feasible, you can break the process down into four half-day meetings, the equivalent of two days.

Thus if you are working with a team of more than seven people, I suggest that you separate participants into more than one group when you arrive at step 7, drafting the vision statement. Each subgroup then works to write its own separate vision statement.

You can then synthesize the multiple vision statements into one statement as follows:

1. Ask each small group to write its vision on flipchart paper and present it to the entire team.

2. Ask the members of each small group to indicate which words, phrases, or sentences in their vision statement they feel strongly about including in the final statement.

3. Underline these words, phrases, and sentences.

4. Rewrite them on separate flipchart pages.

5. Facilitate the large group in creating a vision statement that synthesizes all of these various words, phrases, and statements.

You can then have the large group continue with step 8, refining the executive vision statement. I recommend that at this stage you also obtain input on your vision statement from associates and employees who are not on the team. That will allow you not only to communicate the content of the statement but also to obtain commitment from others.

If you have faithfully gone through all of the exercises in this chapter, you are no doubt finding that you have created a transformation within your team. You started out with a problem, and now you have a vision statement that goes beyond it and inspires you to think more broadly about how to improve your workplace. In my experience with building solutions, this is one of the most exciting aspects of problem solving! I have seen work groups start from zero and end up with an inspiring vision statement and a lot of enthusiasm. The following chapter will provide you with the nuts-and-bolts for creating ideas.

Points to Remember

- A vision is the ideal outcome that you desire for your challenge over the next five to ten years.

- Your vision statement incorporates what you most desire for your problem, as well as ways in which your dreams, passions, skills, and talents may find greater expression as a result of the solution.

- Vision statements are powerful because they point the way to new possibilities, inspire commitment among team members, establish priorities, and lead to agreement for action.

- Developing a vision statement is primarily an intuitive and right-brain activity, and techniques such as visualization can be helpful in stimulating creativity.

- Completing your vision statement with your team is an exciting and rewarding experience and one that benefits from facilitation.

- Your vision statement must be concise, simple, and understandable by everyone on your team and in your organization. It's really a work in progress and will continue to evolve as time goes on.

Chapter Six

Creating Ideas

So deep is the creative spirit that you will never
discover its limits even if you search every trail.
—*Heraclitus*

You now have a vision statement—one that is extensive enough to
point the way to larger improvements for your challenge and possibly also for the organization as a whole. How can you best use that
vision statement so that it does not just become a set of platitudes
that get stuck on a wall or tossed into people's desks and forgotten
about?

The step that most problem-solving processes overlook is the
very necessary one of translating the vision statement for your
problem into discrete, concrete projects. This chapter will therefore show you how to use your vision to carve out such projects.
You will then identify a feasible first project, which solves your original problem, promises maximum results, and gets you closer to
your vision. Finally, it will show you how to generate multiple creative solution ideas for accomplishing your project's goals.

Creativity

Do you believe in your own creativity and the creativity of others?
The first thing you and your team need to do at this stage, poised as
you are to begin the nitty-gritty process of developing solutions, is
to affirm your tremendous capacity for creative thinking. Popular

belief holds that creativity is the province of only a select few individuals. Yet innovation experts will tell you that creativity is an ability that lies within all of us.

Unfortunately, many of us have our creative capabilities thwarted by parents and teachers who may have discouraged us from thinking expansively. The climate in the schools many of us attended and later in the bureaucratic organizations we work in further serves to make us think and behave in rule-bound and pre-scribed ways. As a result, many of us lose touch with the spark of inspiration—and even genius—that resides within us.

So we need to restore our faith in our own creativity and that of others. In my work with communities, organizations, and teams, I have consistently seen people respond in extraordinarily ingenious ways when given the right tools, some encouragement, and a suitable environment. Creativity emerges in activities ranging from putting together a business proposal or developing a marketing brochure to devising a strategic plan or designing a new work process. Indeed, I have seen teams fill reams and reams of flipchart paper with lists of innovative problem-solving ideas.

One thing that helps me personally is the belief that our Higher Power has endowed each of us with all of the creativity we need to improve ourselves, our organizations, our communities, and our planet. So often I find that as soon as we take the first step of trusting our own creative spirit, the Higher Power comes to our aid in the form of strength, support, resources, personal connections, and the tools we need to achieve our goals and realize our vision. Can you remember a time when you moved into that creative space inside yourself and suddenly found that things you needed began easily—even miraculously—coming to you? Dipping into the river of creativity allows us to experience what psychologist Mihaly Csik-szentmihaly calls "flow," that state of consciousness in which we become so involved in what we are doing that nothing else seems to matter and everything seems natural and effortless.

You started to visit the creative space inside yourself in Chapter Five when you looked into your desires, passions, and dreams and how they might find expression in the ultimate solution of your problem. The rest of this chapter will take you further along that path.

Keeping It Fun

Years ago, I visited Imagilab in Lausanne, Switzerland. This is a research organization dedicated to the study and practice of creativity. Imagilab is the home of a unique methodology that has top executives use LEGO bricks to stimulate their creativity as a part of their process to design corporate strategy. Imagilab is capitalizing on the notion of serious play—play that is important, purposeful, and often transformational—to help people think about their tasks in new ways. Clearly, nothing inspires creativity like fun.

Thus it is important that when you and your team work together to create ideas, you maintain a sense of fun. According to creativity expert Roger Von Oech, humor can be a potent stimulus for idea generation. He has found that group members generate more ideas when they are having a good time. In contrast, when participants are serious and become judgmental of themselves and others, creativity suffers. The Greek philosopher Plato verbalized this very concept thousands of years ago when he said, "What, then, it is the right way of living? Life must be lived as play."

I encourage you to approach the exercises in this chapter and in the remainder of this book as you would games. When you engage in them with this attitude, you'll find creativity coming to your team much more easily and solutions falling more readily into place.

Turning Your Vision into Concrete Projects

It's now time to look at the vision statement that you and your team developed to see how you can apply it to specific projects that allow you to address your challenge in concrete terms.

The scope of your vision statement will vary with the nature of the problem it addresses. If your problem is not very complex or relatively small, your vision statement may guide you to develop a project that is limited in scope, such as redesigning a small front office, improving an existing software system, or creating a new office layout.

However, if your problem is larger and more comprehensive, chances are your vision constitutes a broad statement that needs to be broken down into multiple concrete projects that can be carried out as a part of the solution process over the long term. Consider the vision statement of Glass Deco (see Exhibit 6.1). This statement pointed to multiple projects that the organization needed to undertake as part of addressing the original issue of achieving teamwork among the executives. The team took some time to tease out what those projects were and came up with the following:

- Establishing clear mechanisms and procedures to improve cooperation, communication, and problem solving across functions
- Instituting a new reward and recognition system that puts the company's goals first while also allowing departmental goals to be met
- Developing more innovative products
- Improving product quality
- Increasing profitability

After listing the various projects on which they could embark, the members of the Glass Deco team discussed each of them. They then chose to focus on the one that would solve the original problem and would yield the best results in both the short and the long run: establishing clear mechanisms and procedures for cooperation, communication, and problem solving across departments. They all agreed that completing this project would not only be feasible but would also bring them closer to their ultimate vision. It would allow them to achieve integration across different departments and respond effectively to client demands. They would be able to improve

---

Exhibit 6.1 Glass Deco Executive Team Vision Statement

- We work as a team to create the most innovative, most beautiful, and highest-quality glass products in the industry.

- We work collaboratively to achieve Glass Deco's goals for profitability, revenue, and customer satisfaction.

- We cooperate, communicate, and solve problems across functions.

- We are recognized and rewarded for our work in meeting the company's goals as well as the goals of our own departments.

---

the company's profitability, reinvigorate product development practices, and enhance product quality.

Their strategy—starting with one feasible project that solves the original problem, promises maximum results, and gets the team closer to its vision—is a good one for you and your team to adopt as well. Nothing can sabotage your problem-solving process faster than using your vision statement to implement too many projects at once or to engage in projects that are tremendously complex but do not produce results. As a manager, if you get overambitious, you may not realistically be able to follow up on the multiple courses you have set for yourself, your team, and your organization. As a result, you'll end up being perceived as "talking the talk but not walking the walk."

However, you may find that it makes sense to start with more than one project. For example, the Glass Deco team asked human resources to begin working on a second project as well: instituting a new reward system that places an emphasis on both organizational and departmental goals. Not only would this be essential for fostering team spirit, but the new system would also give executive members an additional incentive to work together as a team to achieve the company's overall goals.

It is important that you choose your first project or projects wisely. In the exercises that follow, I will guide you to break your vision statement into discrete projects, prioritize them, and select the undertaking that seems to be the most logical starting point. I recommend that you and your team work with a facilitator to help you with this process, particularly if you are inclined toward starting with more than one project at the same time.

To assist you in prioritizing your projects appropriately, your facilitator will guide you to discuss each project by using the following open-ended questions:

- What is the expected payoff of this project in the short term?
- How can this project move us closer to achieving our vision in the most effective way?
- Does this project solve our original problem?
- How feasible is this project, given our time and budget limitations?

Your facilitator will also guide your team to discuss other topics such as political issues that you may need to consider. Political issues may include such matters as the desires of powerful individuals inside or outside the organization. Once you discuss each of the projects, you will prioritize them and select your first undertaking.

Brainstorming Revisited

Your team will rely on the technique of brainstorming for completing the exercises in this chapter. We took a brief look at brainstorming in Chapter Four. Let's expand on it a bit here.

Say you had been invited to a meeting to help come up with ideas for improving the front office operations of your organization. You were excited to participate and came in with several ideas about how to update the office's image and make it run more efficiently. But the minute you offered your first thoughtful suggestion to the group, the leader shot your idea down and then completely ignored you. How long would it be before you offered another suggestion?

Some people are not fazed by this kind of criticism, but most people find it uncomfortable at best and devastating at worst. In fact, when their ideas are criticized in a group, most people just shut down. The result is, of course, a loss of creativity, innovation, and productivity for the entire team.

Brainstorming is powerful because it takes place in a completely nonjudgmental environment in which everyone's ideas are welcomed, encouraged, and accepted as valid. In this kind of open and safe atmosphere, people tend to relax, think in new and expansive ways, and feel comfortable sharing their thoughts with the group. This is the kind of working environment you want to establish in order to maximize your team's creativity. Doing so not only stimulates individual creativity but also allows a group synergy to develop in which people can bounce ideas back and forth and build on them. This triggers the sigma effect, in which the whole becomes greater than the sum of its parts.

To recap from Chapter Four, brainstorming requires effective facilitation. The facilitator guides the group to do all of the following:

- Devise a clear objective for the brainstorming session
- Rapidly generate as many ideas as possible
- Encourage the participation of all members
- Welcome all ideas
- Prohibit judgment, criticism, or discussion of any ideas at this stage
- Offer further ideas that relate to or enlarge on previously mentioned ideas

The facilitator or recorder make the ideas visible by recording them on flipchart pages that are displayed so that everyone can read them. At the end of the brainstorming session, the group members take a short break. They then get back together to discuss their ideas and select the best ones by using the prioritization technique (see Chapters Four and Seven for additional information on prioritization).

I have never participated in or conducted a brainstorming session that was anything less than both exciting and effective. Attending to some extra details can make these sessions even more fruitful. For example, you need to make sure that the objective of your brainstorming session is well defined. Well-formulated objectives are specific and understood by everyone and do not focus on more than one issue or question.

For example, a goal for a brainstorming session is something like "To come up with ideas for as many projects as possible that seem to emerge from our vision statement" or, as might be appropriate for exercises later in the chapter, "To come up with as many ideas as possible for how we might increase profits by 20 percent in the next year." It *cannot* be something like "To come up with as many ideas as possible for how we might increase profits by 20 percent in the next year *and* how we might reduce turnover." This kind of objective combines two separate issues, and both should not be addressed in the same brainstorming session. With these parameters, you'll find that the ideal brainstorming session will run around forty-five to sixty minutes. This does not include the time you later spend discussing and prioritizing solution ideas.

You can also further spur the creation of a huge quantity of ideas by displaying empty flipcharts all over the room. You may even want to set a goal for the minimum number of ideas to be suggested. Participants will often keep going beyond that goal until all the flipcharts are full.

Moreover, it is important that those present in the meeting, particularly managers, avoid restricting participants' creativity by putting boundaries (such as budget or schedule limitations) on ideas. Such boundaries impede creativity and really belong to the later stages of problem solving, which we will discuss in the coming chapters.

Finally, you may find that your "brainstorms" are becoming stale. In that case, think about the following questions:

- Do you have too much agreement in your team?
- Do participants avoid discussing difficult issues?

If you answer yes, it is time to rock the boat. What you have on your hands is "groupthink," the enemy of creativity. Innovation experts such as Robert Sutton, a professor at Stanford University, prescribe bringing new blood to the team to enhance idea generation and innovation. You can involve people such as these:

- "Devil's advocates" whose natural style is to present completely different points of view
- Participants who are new to the team and the way things are done and are not afraid to express their opinions
- Individuals who are interested in the problem but come from completely unrelated fields

As you are rocking the boat, you will find that brainstorming sessions become richer in ideas. On the other hand, you will need skillful facilitation to manage disagreements effectively.

You are now ready to begin turning your vision statement into a set of concrete projects. Exercise 6.1 will help your team do so.

Exercise 6.1: Identifying Your First Project

Step 1: Breaking Your Vision Statement into Projects

As a team, look at your vision statement. Brainstorm as many distinct projects as possible that could be created out of that vision statement.

Step 2: Discussing the Various Projects

Your facilitator guides your team to discuss each project by using the following four questions:

- What is the expected payoff of this project in the short term?
- How can this project move us closer to achieving our vision in the most effective way?
- Does this project solve our original problem?
- How feasible is the project, given our time and budget limitations?

Other issues that your team considers important are also discussed at this point.

Step 3: Prioritizing Your Projects and Selecting Your First Undertaking

Now that you have a clearer understanding about your projects, you can prioritize them based on your discussion. Your facilitator will ask each of you to select the one or two most crucial projects, you will all cast your votes in round-robin fashion, and the tallies will be recorded next to each item. You will then be able to discover what your team deems to be the most favored projects and will select your first undertaking on that basis.

Defining Your Project's Goals

Now that you've selected your first project aimed at solving your original problem and moving toward your ultimate vision, you need to come up with specific goals for it. Setting goals is very important, for without them your project will suffer from a lack of focus.

Your *goal statements* reflect what you want to accomplish with your project in terms that are *specific, measurable,* and *time-limited.*

Categories at which goals are aimed typically include one or more of the following:

Profitability

Market share

Productivity

Customer satisfaction

Innovation

Quality

Employee responsibilities

Turnover

I also recommend developing goals that have been tracked or are easy to track over time so that your team can make meaningful and objective project evaluation comparisons (see also Chapter Eight). You can then measure current performance levels and use them as baseline figures.

For example, as mentioned earlier, the members of the Glass Deco executive team chose as their first project "To improve teamwork by establishing clear mechanisms and procedures for cooperation, communication, and problem solving across departments." They decided to measure the impact of this project through its effect on the company's profitability and on customer satisfaction. They therefore developed the following goals for this project:

- To increase overall profitability by 10 percent within a year
- To improve the customer satisfaction index by 10 percent within a year

They also chose these goals because the company had been tracking both profitability and customer satisfaction on a quarterly basis for quite a while. This meant that they would be able to use the current levels of profitability and customer satisfaction as baselines to which they would compare their future performance a year hence.

Exercise 6.2 will help you define the goals for your first project.

Exercise 6.2: Setting Goals for Your Project

Develop two or three solid goal statements that reflect what you hope to accomplish with your first project. Remember that they need to be specific, measurable, and time limited. Also make sure that these goals have been or can be measured prior to the start of the project.

Developing a Long-Term View

Be sure to save the list of the other projects your team has come up with. Doing so will allow your group to keep in mind a long-range vision for your problem while you go about working on the first project.

Exercise 6.3: Saving a Portfolio of Projects

On flipchart paper visible to everyone in the room, provide a clean list of the other projects your team came up with in Exercise 6.2. Have someone retain that list for the future.

Creating Ideas

So now you have developed some specific goals—the first concrete outcomes you wish to accomplish as you start transforming the challenge you identified in Chapter One into an opportunity. How do you and your team make these goals a reality?

As we discussed, your next step is to come up with lots of creative ideas to help turn these goals into opportunities. The rest of this chapter will discuss techniques to help you do just that. These exercises are designed, once again, to stimulate the right brain and help you break out of the box that our logical thinking tends to impose. I've found these activities to be exciting and useful in my own personal projects and in my work with organizations. These techniques can generally be used both by individuals and groups.

My aim is to help you come up with lots of ideas so that you can go beyond solutions that are merely "adequate" and reach for those that are truly outstanding. I also wish to help you and your team expand your capacity for generating creative ideas, in general, as this skill will be broadly translatable in other areas and will greatly enhance your individual and collective productivity.

Association

The mind works by the principle of association. This means that anytime you have an idea, you automatically tend to associate it with another similar or different idea. The ancient Greeks articulated the laws of association, noting specifically that when you think of an idea, your mind often triggers something that is "near," "similar to," or "opposite" that idea.

For example, when you think of a movie screen, you may think of something located "near" that object, such as a theater seat. Or you may think of something "similar to" a movie screen, such as a television screen. You may also think of something that is "opposite" in nature to a movie screen, such as a live performance.

You can capitalize on the natural activity of association to come up with ideas for your project. You start with a word and then let your mind suggest as many other "near," "similar," and "opposite" concepts related to that word as possible. As they come up, record them on paper. For example, say that your project goal is to create a new, fun-oriented product line. To generate some ideas for ways to achieve that goal, you might start with the word *fun* and then write down as many ideas and concepts as possible that are associated with it. Words such as *play, toys, kids, love, gym, joy, light, sun, beach, clothes, sandals,* and *walking* might emerge. Then look at all the words that have come to the surface and see if they point to any ideas that make sense for your business line.

Free Association

If association is effective for generating ideas, free association can be even more so. In free association, you start with a word (thought, concept, or idea) and come up with as many others as you can that may be related *or unrelated* to it. You can also begin a free association activity by picking a word that has come to you in the form of a hunch or simply by picking a word at random from the dictionary and brainstorming around that.

The following exercise is most successful when it's done quickly without too much conscious thought. The point is to let your unconscious mind take over. That's where all of your creative ideas lie.

The free association exercise can be done by you alone, but it is extremely powerful when it is done with a group. That's because team members will start exchanging and building on each other's ideas, fueling a productive synergy. The following exercise helps you use this technique to work on your project by forcing an association with a couple of key words that describe your project best.

Exercise 6.4: Free Association Exercise

This exercise is designed for a group, but it can also be done by individuals.

Look over the description of the project and project goals you have come up with based on your vision statement. Write a one- or two-word summary of it at the top of a page of flipchart paper in front of the room.

Summary: _____

Below that heading on the flipchart, write the numbers 1 through 15 in a column. Have any team member randomly throw out one word or idea that comes to mind based on the summary word. Then have the team look at the word on line 1 and similarly throw out any related or unrelated word that comes to mind, which is then written on line 2. Continue until you have at least fifteen words (you needn't stop at fifteen). For best results, this should be done in rapid-fire fashion without too much thinking.

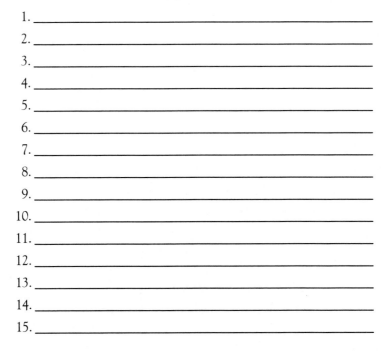

1. _____
2. _____
3. _____
4. _____
5. _____
6. _____
7. _____
8. _____
9. _____
10. _____
11. _____
12. _____
13. _____
14. _____
15. _____

When you have finished, review all of the words or ideas that you have written down. Do any of them suggest further ideas or directions for your project and for achieving your project's goals? Record your team's ideas on flipchart pages that are visible to everyone.

Metaphors

A *metaphor* is a figure of speech that expresses how one thing is like another. (If it uses the word *like* or *as,* it is known as a *simile.*) For example, in the movie *Forrest Gump,* Forrest makes the following metaphorical statement: "Life is like a box of chocolates. You never know what you're going to get." He is thus using the metaphor of a box of chocolates to talk about life.

We use metaphors all the time. For example, we commonly use sports metaphors to talk about business concepts: "step up to the plate," "he's a real team player," "that's out of the ballpark." We sometimes use the metaphor of the human circulatory system to describe the layout of the buildings and roads within our cities. And we use the metaphor of the pump to describe the workings of the heart.

Metaphors, which are based on the principle of association and are poetic creations of the right brain, can be used to better understand our situations, gain insights, and generate new ideas. You can use them to view your project in new ways.

For example, if your goal is "To increase sales by 20 percent by the end of the year," one metaphor you might come up with is that increasing sales by 20 percent "is like climbing to the top of a mountain" or "is like running a marathon." I was recently involved with a project in which representatives from three departments—customer service, marketing and sales, and order fulfillment—were thinking of ways to work better as a team. The group came up with two metaphors about their project: "Our goal is to operate as an NBA championship team" and "Our goal is to work together seamlessly."

The group members then compared their project with the first metaphor. They decided that in order to operate as an NBA championship team, they would need to define (1) what each department is best at (establish clear roles and responsibilities) and (2) in which areas they could get assistance from the other departments. They then moved on to the second metaphor, which led them to identify the best ways in which they could support each other without any special coordination mechanisms. Such special mechanisms include written or verbal requests and cross-departmental meetings. After implementing these suggestions, they are now better coordinated, their sales are up by 10 percent, and their customer satisfaction index has improved dramatically.

The following exercise guides you to look at your project, come up with metaphors to describe it, and see if any new ideas about it emerge as a result.

Exercise 6.5: Thinking Metaphorically

This activity should be done with your team, but you can also do it alone.

Consider the project and the goals that you are about to tackle. On flipchart paper in front of the room, write up to five metaphors that describe it.

1.

2.

3.

4.

5.

Compare your project or your goals with one of these metaphors, answering the following questions:

What similarities do you see between the two?

What additional insights about your project or your goals does this metaphor provide you?

Can you think of any new ideas about how you might carry out your project or achieve your goals as a result of these insights?

Sleep and Dreams

Do you know that sleep holds some of the best answers to our problems? It is during sleep and in our dreams that our unconscious mind is allowed free rein and can come up with the most amazing ideas.

I can attest to this fact based on personal experience. Since I was young, I have found sleep and dreams to be a source of many ideas for my school projects and, later, numerous successful business projects. I regularly get many ideas for writing winning business and grant proposals in my dreams. My dreams have even provided me with inspiration for several sections of this book. When I am making an important decision, my dreams similarly provide me with breakthrough insights. For instance, when I was looking for a new home, I had a dream in which I was endlessly driving around town and listening to the radio until I was finally directed to approach the street where I found my current home. Go figure!

Evidence for the importance of dreams comes from many different fields, including history, art, literature, religion, and science. Thomas Edison, for example, used brief periods of sleep to stimulate his creativity. The Russian chemist Dmitri Mendeleyev was inspired by his dreams to put together the periodic table. Friedrich August Kekulé created the benzene molecule based on inspiration that came to him in a dream. And the famous composer Hector Berlioz got ideas for his *Symphonie Fantastique* from a dream.

Sometimes the messages in your dreams are amazingly loud and clear. Yet most times (when you are able remember your dreams at all), the ideas you recall may seem irrelevant and unrelated to what you're trying to accomplish. Nevertheless, you can still use the symbols and scenarios that show up to stimulate your imagination. When you try to make sense of your dreams, you are engaging in a type of creative thinking. Dream analysis is an association technique in which you are trying to make a connection between the information you have received and your current challenge. In fact, experts recommend a whole series of activities to capitalize on your dreams, which are included in the following exercise.

So your dreams are a valuable tool for discovering solutions! You will find that they frequently contain hints or clues that will inspire you and your team members to create new ideas for your project.

Exercise 6.6: Getting Ideas from a Dream

Think about your project before going to sleep.

Create an affirmation for yourself, such as, "I will receive guidance about my project tonight, and I will remember all relevant dreams when I wake up." Strengthen that affirmation by repeating it several times mentally, saying it out loud, or writing it down just before going to bed.

When you wake up, in the morning or in the middle of the night, take a moment to remember what you were dreaming about before doing anything else. Lie there quietly with your eyes closed until something comes to you. You could also write down your dream in a journal or on note cards.

1. Make careful note of any ideas and solutions regarding your project that may be embedded in your dream.

2. Take one of the objects, concepts, symbols, or ideas in your dream. Spend five minutes doing a free association with it.

Asking "What If . . . ?"

Asking questions that begin with "What if . . ." is one of the most powerful ways of stimulating your creativity. "What if" questions give you permission to imagine what your situation would be like or what might happen if the assumptions and limitations about your situation did not exist. The broadest kind of "what if" questions might be things like "What if everyone were motivated at work?" "What if creating any system were possible?" and—one that you have already used in devising your vision statement—"What if we had all the resources in the world?"

At this stage, you'll want to turn the "what if" activity to your current project and project goals. For example, one question you come up with might be "What if we had an unlimited budget for achieving our goals?"

Exercise 6.7: "What If . . . ?"

Look at your current project and project goals. As a team, come up with at least three "what if" questions that would allow you to remove limitations and think in new ways about how you might achieve your goals.

List your three questions:

1.

2.

3.

Then have your team brainstorm ideas for achieving your goals as though each of these "what if" questions were true. (Save these ideas for use in Chapter Seven.)

Taking a Break

Another technique that helps stimulate creativity is simply taking a break. Sometimes this can be a short break, and other times it may be an extended break.

I personally like to immerse myself in a project and all the information associated with it for a certain period of time. Then I just take some time off. This gives me a chance to put things in perspective. And I often find that while I'm away, doing things unrelated to my problem, opportunity appears. It's almost as though all the information that is in my head spontaneously starts to organize itself and generate new ideas.

For example, at one point I was working on a presentation about cross-cultural issues for a specific client. After examining the needs and desires of my client, I immersed myself in reading various books and presentations other colleagues had made about cross-cultural issues. Then I took the afternoon off. Suddenly, the basis of my entire presentation came into my mind without my having to make any effort at all.

So I recommend that you have your team immerse itself in meetings about your project and then postpone doing anything further on the issue for several days or even a couple of weeks, if you can afford the time. At that point, come back together and discuss what ideas have come to you in the interim.

Deadlines

I honestly don't know what it is about deadlines, but they certainly can light a fire under people and push them on to creative breakthroughs. As I was writing this book, for example, my publisher and I set up various deadlines for each chapter. I found that as I was working against each one of these deadlines, more and more ideas kept coming to me. I know that without such deadlines, this book would never have come into being!

The most successful grant writer I have ever met works on many projects simultaneously and is therefore juggling multiple deadlines. She has an amazing success rate: over 70 percent of the grant proposals that she has written to date have been funded. She too admits that deadlines play a major role in keeping her creative juices flowing.

Exercise 6.8: Setting Deadlines

Write the column headings "Milestones" and "Deadlines" at the top of a sheet of paper. With your team, write down three important milestones for your projects that you definitely want to complete. Then establish a deadline for each of the milestones.

Milestones	*Deadlines*
1.	
2.	
3.	

Visualization

Another technique that works extremely well for generating ideas is visualization. You learned how to use visualization in Chapter Five, when you applied it to crafting a vision statement. You can turn to it again to help you come up with ideas for bringing your project goals into reality.

To do this, you will want to revisit the instructions and exercises in Chapter Five and Appendix C. To recap, either working alone or with your team, you'll want to calm your mind and body through relaxation and meditation and then engage in a visualization in which you have already achieved those goals and are living them. The next exercise will help you apply the visualization exercise to this stage of your problem-solving journey.

Exercise 6.9: Visualizing for Your Project

Have a facilitator take you through the team visualization in Appendix C, replacing the words "You suddenly see in front of you somebody who can give you all the insight you need to turn your problem around" with the following:

"You are suddenly in a situation in which you have already achieved your project goals."

The facilitator continues the visualization with the following:

"What do you see?
"What are you doing?
"What are others doing? How are they behaving?
"How do you feel?
"What ideas are coming to you?
"Now come slowly back into the room and gently open your eyes."

Have your team members write down answers to the following questions:

Do you have any new insights and ideas about how you may achieve your project goals as a result of your visualization?

Pick a word, image, or idea that came to you during your visualization. Spend five minutes doing a free association with it. Write down all of the words that come to you.

What further insights, about your project goals and how to achieve them, come to you as a result of looking at your free association list?

Affirmations

As we discussed in Chapter Two, affirmations are positive statements you generate about your situation and repeat over and over to yourself in order to begin manifesting them as reality. Remember that these statements should be formulated in the present tense, as though what you want to achieve has already come to pass.

For example, if one of your project goals is "To increase profits by 20 percent in the next year," some of your related affirmations may be "We now have all of the resources we need to increase our profits by 20 percent in the next year" and "We are now generating 20 percent more in profits that we were last year." Although this activity may seem unrealistic and even silly, don't underestimate its power to influence reality. At the very least, you'll find that having your team develop various affirmations about your project goals and keep them visible around the office will further stimulate creative ideas and will generate positive momentum for your project.

Exercise 6.10: Creating Affirmations for Your Project

Have your team create five affirmations about your project and your project goals.

1.

2.

3.

4.

5.

Brainstorming Yet Again

In addition to engaging in all of the previous exercises to help stimulate ideas for realizing your project goals, you will of course want to engage in one or several sessions in which you use the time-tested technique of brainstorming.

When you have finished working through the activities in this chapter, you should have a sea of ideas before you for how you can begin to bring your first project to fruition. The next chapter will help you sift through all of these ideas and craft your actual solution.

Points to Remember

- Creativity is a capacity we all possess.

- Approaching the steps involved in generating ideas as an enjoyable game will yield the most creative results.

- To keep your vision statement from becoming a list of meaningless platitudes, you must break it into specific projects.

- Start with a project that is feasible, solves the original problem, promises maximum results, and gets the team closer to its vision. But don't be overambitious; make it something that your team can realistically handle.

- Once you have selected the first project, establish several specific, measurable goals.

- Use the techniques of brainstorming, free association, metaphors, dream analysis, asking "what if," breaks, deadlines, visualization, and affirmations to generate ideas for turning your project goals into reality.

Chapter Seven

Developing the Solution

I keep six honest serving men (they taught me all I know);
Their names are what and why and when and how and
where and who.

—*Rudyard Kipling*

You and your team are now standing in front of an ocean of ideas
for your first project that you generated in Chapter Six. Somewhere
in that ocean lies the right combination of ideas that will serve as
the ideal solution for your challenge and will get you closer to your
vision. What you need to do now is sort out those particular ideas
from the rest.

Your group may be both excited and uneasy about what lies
ahead. You're probably asking questions like these:

How will our team be able to turn these ideas into an effective solution that will be acceptable to all players?

Will we make the right decisions?

What if things change and the vision changes?

Will the solution that we choose take us in the right
direction?

These questions—and your uncertainty—are normal. Remember
the positive thinking tools from Chapter Two? This is the time
when all of those tools will again come in handy. You can revisit

them to generate the excitement and inner strength that will propel you to put together the best solution. In particular, the Believing Game and the Positive Inventory are your best allies in getting through these moments of insecurity. I regularly use them with teams at this stage. So go back and use these tools again, both on your own and with your team members!

This chapter will help your team to develop the solution by guiding you through three steps, as shown in Figure 7.1. In the first step, "Create Alternatives," you will sort through the ideas that you generated in Chapter Six by using techniques such as prioritizing and grouping in order to develop a number of solution alternatives. In the second step, "Make Decisions," you will select the solution you think is best. This step involves learning about methods for achieving consensus among team members. Finally, in the third step, "Refine the Solution," you'll have a chance to improve your selected solution and make it as workable as possible.

Combining Ideas into Alternatives

The first step in developing your solution is to look back at all of the great ideas you generated in Chapter Six and combine them into solution alternatives. You may for a moment question this activity,

Figure 7.1 Developing the Solution

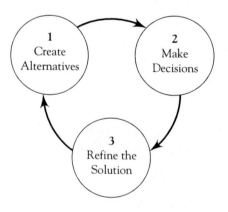

thinking that you have already gathered all the ideas you need. Yet individual ideas are rarely broad enough to serve as complete, full-blown solutions. Alternatives combine a number of ideas. They are broad enough to provide a complete blueprint for accomplishing your project. Moreover, you want to develop several such complete solution alternatives. You will then pick the alternative that is both the most viable and the most focused on achieving excellence.

You can think of an alternative as an entire car and an idea as its engine. Without the engine, the car does not function. But an engine is only part of what makes a car a complete transportation vehicle.

Let's look at an example, a simple project that sought to build excellence in supervision at a manufacturing plant. An idea was to provide supervisory skills training to a select group of managers. This idea needed further development in order to become a full solution alternative. It failed to take into account the following questions:

> What aspects of supervisory skills would be addressed during training?
>
> Which of these aspects would be emphasized, based on the needs of these managers?
>
> How would the program transfer skills into practice so that the training would stick and result in improved performance?
>
> What additional systemic changes did the organization have to make in order to allow these individuals to excel in supervision?

The full solution needed to address all of these questions as well. Therefore, the alternative that the group selected pointed to the various aspects of supervisory skills that would be included in the training, such as leadership, rewards and motivation, strategic planning, team building, communication, and cross-cultural issues. The team members also decided to make communication, team building, and problem solving the primary emphases of the training. Moreover, they included in their solution two additional components in order to transfer skills to the workplace. First, the plant would set up a coaching system for the supervisors whereby they would continue to receive support from their senior peers on an ongoing basis. Second, the organization would establish a system of rewards for supervisors in order to reinforce expected behaviors and performance.

Can you now see how an *alternative* differs from an *idea*? Alternatives combine several ideas and provide full-blown solutions for what you are trying to accomplish.

Now you are ready to put together your alternatives.

Prioritizing Revisited and Expanded

Prioritizing is an activity that allows your team to determine what its most favored ideas are for your first project from among those you have generated up to this point. As we discussed previously, prioritizing follows the idea generation stage of brainstorming. Facilitators use this method to support teams in sorting through the ideas that they generated during the brainstorming sessions. Let's review the steps:

1. The facilitator asks the team members to select their "top" ideas, usually between three and five ideas. Each situation is unique, however, so facilitators may adjust the number of top choices accordingly. Sometimes, for instance, I may ask group members to choose their "top" one or two ideas (especially at the stage in which the team is choosing its first project, as we saw in Chapter Six). Moreover, if participants feel that they need to work with more choices, I go ahead and offer them the freedom to do so.

2. Each participant votes for his or her top ideas in round-robin fashion while the facilitator or recorder marks the votes next to each item on the flipchart pages.

3. The facilitator or recorder then counts the scores for the various ideas. The items with the highest votes easily stand out at this point. These are recorded on a new set of flipchart pages.

A nice alternative to this method is to give team members "participation dots"—self-adhesive dots that can be found in any office supply store. The number each team member is given depends on the number of top ideas that each person may select. The facilitator then asks each person to stand up and place the dots next to his or her favorite ideas on the flipchart paper. The facilitator counts the dots, and the ideas with the highest number of dots are recorded on a new set of flipchart pages. This method generates a lot of activity and really engages the participants. I personally find it more effective than simply voting in round-robin fashion.

After prioritizing, you may ask, "What will we do with the rest of the ideas we generated? Are we going to forget about them?" Not at all! In fact, you need to hang on to all of your ideas because you will use them later to possibly enlarge your alternatives and make them even more creative and attractive. So ask your minute taker to type up all the ideas, along with the number of votes they received, and distribute them to all team members.

You are now ready to engage in the first exercise of this chapter, which will guide you and your team in prioritizing your ideas.

Exercise 7.1: Prioritizing Your Ideas

1. Call a meeting in which you display all the ideas for your first project from your brainstorming sessions of Chapter Six on flipchart pages. The pages are taped all over the room so that the ideas are visible to everyone. Sometimes you may have all walls full of ideas!

2. The facilitator asks team members to select their "top" items from the list (usually between three and five ideas).

3. Each team member votes in round-robin fashion while the facilitator or recorder places checks or ticks beside each idea that is selected. Checks or ticks should be recorded in a color different from the one in which the ideas themselves are written. Alternatively, you may have team members vote by placing colored adhesive dots next to their top choices.

4. The facilitator counts the votes, and the ideas with the highest votes are revealed. The team decides which ideas are the most crucial. The facilitator or the recorder then writes down the team's top ideas on a new set of flipchart pages. The pages are clearly displayed.

Grouping Ideas into Solution Alternatives

The next step is to group your top choices into several solution alternatives for your project. Grouping is actually something that our mind naturally tends to do. That's because most of us can only hold around six or seven information items in our heads at any given time. As a result, we automatically sort multiple ideas into categories in order to be able to manage all the information at our disposal more effectively. I therefore instruct teams to optimize this natural tendency by grouping ideas not merely to organize the information but also to formulate viable solution alternatives.

Grouping is the process of taking your list of ideas and putting them together into thematic groupings or like categories. As a rule of thumb, grouping is usually necessary when prioritization has yielded more than ten "best" items. Once the process is complete, you usually end up with three to five groupings. Sometimes, however, you may end up with as many as eight groupings. Your team then works with each group of ideas to devise a solution alternative. The process is usually as follows:

1. The facilitator asks team members to think about logical thematic groupings, categories that emerge out of their prioritized ideas.
2. Team members share their ideas about groupings.
3. The facilitator assists the team in agreeing on the various groupings.
4. The discussion continues until all groupings emerge. When there are no more categories and participants agree with

what has emerged, each grouping is given a separate title or heading, which is written down on new flipchart pages.

5. The team works together to turn each grouping into a full solution alternative for the project.

Solution Alternatives at Waferinc

To understand how to group your ideas into alternatives, let's look at how a high-technology manufacturer, Waferinc, generated several solution alternatives for having a superb order-tracking database that supports customer service excellence throughout the company.

Years ago, Waferinc had made a large investment in a new order-tracking information system. Although the new system seemed promising at the beginning, it delivered disappointing results. The company expected to have all employees using the system and thought that this would lead to improved customer satisfaction and increased sales. Instead, however, customer complaints increased and sales stayed flat. Moreover, two years after Waferinc completed the installation and training, many employees were still not using the database.

The vice president, the project's champion and main decision maker, formed a core problem-solving team of nine individuals to address the issue. The group included employees from a wide variety of departments, including the front office, customer service, information systems, the shop floor, and marketing and sales. During the first couple of meetings, the team crafted a simple vision statement for addressing the problem: "We have an information system that supports customer service excellence throughout the company. All employees use the system in order to continuously solve customer problems and achieve high customer satisfaction levels. We are rewarded based on high customer satisfaction levels, high profitability, and increased sales."

Team members then transformed this vision statement into four different projects and selected as their first project "to have a superb order-tracking system database that supports us in achieving customer service excellence throughout the company." They all felt that this was a feasible project that addressed their original problem and promised maximum results while getting them closer to their ultimate vision.

The next gathering was an open forum for generating ideas to achieve their first project. The meeting attracted more than twenty participants. As a facilitator, I was excited to see the enthusiasm with which the participants engaged in the brainstorming session. They ended up generating more than 120 ideas and took a short break. I then worked with the team members to help them prioritize their ideas. They selected the best fifteen out of the bunch (see Exhibit 7.1). Finally, we ended the day and agreed to meet again with the core problem-solving team.

During the subsequent meeting of the core team, I supported the participants to work with their top ideas and combine them into thematic groupings. They formulated and agreed on four groupings or categories of ideas: (1) buying a new system, (2) setting up training and support programs, (3) improving the system internally, and (4) revamping the system by using vendors. They then worked with each of these groupings to turn them into full solution alternatives. For example, the first grouping encompassed ideas 1, 6, 9, and 11 of Exhibit 7.1. They used these ideas to create a short yet cohesive description for their first solution alternative. They continued the process and came up with four different solution alternatives:

Alternative 1: Buy a new system. Discard the existing system. Identify customer needs and wants, and buy a new system that addresses them better. The proposed system would be modular, easy to use, and accessible to everyone in the organization. Use of the system would improve dramatically, and customer service would improve as a result. Finally, the costs of this solution would not be higher than the costs involved in any of the other possible solution alternatives.

Exhibit 7.1 Waferinc's "Best" Ideas
for the Company's First Project

1. Discard the current system and buy a new and better one.

2. Have the information systems department improve the system internally.

3. Find out what needs to be improved about the system.

4. Conduct an assessment to determine why the system is not used.

5. Redesign the training program and train all employees again.

6. Improve the system to make it easy to use and modular.

7. Redesign the system to provide online access for customers. This will enable them to find out about the status of their orders and will lead to higher client satisfaction and increased sales.

8. Have the system track customer preferences.

9. Make the system accessible to everyone in the organization.

10. All departments must be able to use the system to obtain useful information and create customized reports for their own purposes.

11. Define our customers' needs and wants clearly and then customize the new system to meet them.

12. Provide more tools to employees besides training, such as job aids (a short manual with handy instructions, a one-page summary of shortcuts, and so on).

13. Establish a peer support program to provide assistance with using the system anytime employees need it.

14. Revamp the current system completely.

15. Use outside vendors to revamp the current system most effectively.

Alternative 2: Set up training and support programs. The current system is great. We need to conduct an assessment to determine why it is not being used and what skills people need in order to use it properly. We must redesign the training program and offer it to everyone in the organization. We will create job aids (a short manual with helpful hints, for example) for using the system and establish a peer support system whereby employees can receive assistance on an ongoing basis.

Alternative 3: Improve the system internally. Revisit the current system and determine why it is not used and how to improve it. Have the information systems department enhance the system to make it more user-friendly. Making it easier to use would spur more employees to adopt it. Increased use would result in improved customer satisfaction.

Alternative 4: Revamp the system by using vendors. Determine what needs to be improved, and contact various systems development companies, including the original vendor. All these companies will provide proposals and bids to: a) make the system as user-friendly as possible, b) make the system available on the Internet so that customers could access parts of it as well, and c) redesign the system so that departments could have access to customer data at all times, including information about customer needs and wants and about current orders and inquiries. Having access to such data would allow employees to improve how they interact with customers. Moreover, it would allow sales and marketing to better determine customers' need and wants and thereby build closer relationships with them. This would lead to improved customer service and also increased sales.

After grouping the ideas into these four alternatives, the team members discussed them further. They decided to make alternative 2, training and support, a part of all three other alternatives because they realized it would have to be a part of any solution. Thus they ended up with three solid alternative solutions.

You now have seen how Waferinc started by generating 120 ideas, next reduced them to the best fifteen through prioritization, and then grouped these fifteen choices into four and then three solution alternatives. The following exercise will help you facilitate your own grouping session.

Exercise 7.2: Grouping Your Ideas into Solution Alternatives

1. The facilitator asks team members to look at the ideas and think about how to group them together. This can be done by asking an open-ended question, such as "What thematic groupings or categories seem to emerge from your best ideas?"

2. Team members take a stab at identifying thematic categories with the support of the facilitator.

3. Each time a new grouping emerges, the facilitator asks, "Does this sound like a new grouping?" If there is at least basic agreement, the facilitator or recorder then records it on flipchart paper.

4. When there are no more ideas for categories, the facilitator asks some closed-ended questions, such as "Do you all agree with these groupings?" and "Are there any other additional groupings that you want to discuss?" The discussion continues until all the groupings have been defined and participants agree with them.

5. Once groupings have been defined and decided on, the facilitator or recorder writes each one down as the title of a separate flipchart page.

6. The team then works with each grouping of ideas and develops descriptions for each alternative. Participants make certain that each alternative provides a complete solution to what they are trying to accomplish. This step is accomplished faster by assigning different alternatives to individual team members or subgroups. Team members or subgroups then present their work to the entire group.

7. Alternatives are recorded and displayed.

Working with Your Alternatives

You now have your various alternatives in front of you. It's time to improve them and describe them further. First, look to see how you might take the best from each of these alternatives or how you might combine various alternatives to forge even more effective solutions. Second, provide more details to each solution so that you can have a useful comparison during the next step, decision making. There are three avenues you can use to accomplish these goals:

1. The first avenue is to *cross-fertilize* among various alternatives, that is, to incorporate into one of your alternatives ideas from

several of the other alternatives in order to enlarge and enhance it. You can also cross-fertilize by seeing if any of the ideas that were not included as your top choices can be incorporated into one or more of your alternatives.

2. The second avenue is to *merge* two alternatives into one. The resulting solution combines the ideas of both alternatives. Waferinc did this when it merged alternative 2 into each of the other three solutions. As a result, training and support became a part of all of the other solutions. Doing this also allowed the team to focus on a smaller number of alternatives.

3. The third avenue is to *add details* to each one of your alternative solutions. You can use the following questions to do so:

- Who will be involved in developing and implementing this particular solution?
- What needs to be done?
- How will it be done?
- How many working hours are needed to complete the project?
- When will it be completed?
- How much will it cost?
- What are the estimated monetary and nonmonetary benefits of implementing this solution?

You may also want to consider dividing up your team into subgroups and having each of them flesh out a different alternative.

Note that you can spend a lot of time adding details to each alternative, but I would not recommend that you do so at this stage. What I suggest is that you add just enough information to be able to distinguish clearly between the alternatives and make a decision about the best alternative. In other words, at this stage your solution does not have to be completely comprehensive.

The next exercise will help you cross-fertilize, merge, and add details to your alternatives.

Exercise 7.3: Working with Your Alternatives

1. Have your team spend some time cross-fertilizing among your alternatives.

2. Now see if it makes sense to merge any of your alternatives. If so, come up with new descriptions for each alternative that reflect the merging and cross-fertilization. List each alternative on its own piece of flipchart paper, and tape all of them next to one another on a wall in the front of the room.

3. Next, add details to your alternatives by working on the following questions. (You may want to divide up into smaller groups and assign each group to work on a different alternative.)

   • Who will be involved in developing and implementing this solution?
   • What needs to be done?
   • How will it be done?
   • How many working hours are needed to complete the project?
   • When will it be completed?
   • How much will it cost?
   • What are the estimated monetary and nonmonetary benefits of implementing this solution?

4. Summarize your alternatives on flipchart paper at the front of the room.

5. Finally, summarize your alternatives on paper in order to be able to have a solid picture of all of them. You can assign this to your minute taker or to anyone who may volunteer at this stage. Such a visual summary will be very valuable as you go into your next step, decision making. You can use a template like this one:

	Alternative 1	Alternative 2	Alternative 3
Shorthand name			
Brief description			
Estimated time to complete			
Estimated working hours needed			
Estimated cost			
Estimated monetary benefits			
Other details			

Making Decisions

You have now transformed your ideas into several viable, attractive, workable alternatives. At this point, you will select the one that you wish to implement.

Choosing the Solution

Making this decision can often be challenging. You and your team members may find yourselves agonizing over which alternative road to take. Remember that your number one enemy here is fear—fear that you might not make the right decision. I caution you not to let your concerns immobilize you and cause you to put off making the decision. That will only compound your problem.

Several years ago, for example, my colleagues and I were working with a Fortune 500 company that was interested in implementing a large-scale reorganization project. After talking with the client's managers a couple of times, we realized that they had avoided making any changes for at least a year. They had already hired three outside companies to conduct needs assessments for them, and it was clear what they had to do. But they still were not sure that they would be making the right move. They wanted us to validate the results of the previous assessments!

Can we ever be 100 percent sure that we are making the right decision? Of course not. All we can do is make a well-informed choice and move forward. Otherwise we're wasting time and money and missing out on opportunities.

Remember that no matter which alternative you choose, you will have an opportunity to learn. There are really no "winning" or "losing" alternatives. Each one will bring benefits—as well as lessons that you and your team need in order to become even more successful in the future.

And don't underestimate the power of intuition in helping you make your decision. Try to pay attention to your inner voice in selecting your solution—the voice that tells you that one path will be more productive than another or that one path will bring the most exciting and inspiring change. Go with what excites you and what instinctively feels right to you. This is especially true in cases in which your project is about creating something that has never been done before.

Your intuition may even run contrary to the numbers of your analysis. For example, you might be looking at an alternative to create a new product in a new market. The numbers might show that this will be a risky undertaking. Nevertheless, your intuition may tell you that this is the option that sounds the most exciting and the most compatible with your vision. This, then, would be the alternative you should select. Remember what you learned in Chapter Two: things will ultimately turn out fine whatever avenue you choose. Besides, your Higher Power will always be there to support you.

The next exercise asks you to ponder all the advantages that each particular alternative will give you. Its purpose is to fill you with self-confidence and enthusiasm no matter which route you take.

Exercise 7.4: Seeing the Benefits of Each Alternative

1. Again tape all of your alternatives next to one another on flip-chart pages in front of the room. Make sure there is space under each alternative for additional writing. If not, tape a blank piece of flipchart paper under each alternative.

2. Going through each alternative one by one, have your team brainstorm about all of the benefits that the alternative will bring. This can include things such as these:

   • Greater profitability
   • Increased skills
   • Greater job satisfaction
   • Higher customer satisfaction
   • Increased sales
   • Greater market share
   • Better quality

- New knowledge
- Access to new technology
- More innovative product designs

3. Record the benefits of each alternative.

4. Ask a team member or the minute taker to summarize your discussion on a page that can later be distributed to the entire group.

5. Review the results of this exercise along with those of Exercise 7.3. As a group, decide whether a favorite alternative emerges. If so, decide whether you are ready to select this alternative as your final solution.

If your team is not ready to make a decision at this stage, continue reading the rest of this chapter. It will guide you further in evaluating your alternatives and will show you how you can come to group consensus on your final decision.

Understanding Disagreement and Consensus

If your team cannot yet come to a decision as to which solution to pick, you are more than likely experiencing some disagreement among your group. This is a natural part of the decision-making process. Moreover, despite popular belief, disagreement is necessary when you want to arrive at innovative solutions. Ideally, you have already worked through the storming phase of your group process, as discussed in Chapter Three, and you have resolved your interpersonal issues and established norms regarding appropriate and expected behavior. However, this does not mean that all conflict has gone away. It is at this decision-making stage that conflict tends to creep into your group process once more.

So before we go any further, it's important to understand the three main reasons why people disagree. The most frequent reason is that they have not heard and understood each other's point of view. The second reason is that they have differing values, experiences, and backgrounds. And the third reason is that their personalities clash or they have had a difficult history together.

Personality-based conflict is recognizable because it makes participants very emotional. It can take a long time to resolve, and it cannot and should not be dealt with during your decision-making meetings. If it arises, your facilitator needs to deflect it and have the parties address the issues outside the meeting.

You can definitely deal effectively with the other two forms of conflict. At the very least, you can make sure that all team members review the guidelines for effective communication and for keeping the meeting safe (see Chapters Three and Four). In addition, your facilitator can support the team to employ these techniques at this stage. As a result, group members will be able to listen actively, respect each other's values and viewpoints, and understand each other. By identifying what everyone has in common, your team will begin to build consensus around the final decision.

Achieving consensus means obtaining basic agreement from every single member of the team that a given decision is the right one. This is your purpose no matter what solution you ultimately choose. Note that consensus is different from majority rule. In majority rule, up to 49 percent of the participants may not agree with the final decision and may even strongly oppose it. This is not what you want when it comes to picking your solution, because having people who are not favorable toward it can cause serious problems during the planning and implementation stages. You want to be sure that everyone accepts the solution. This does not necessarily mean that everyone will be ecstatic about the decision. It means that *everyone understands the selected solution, can live with it, and will support it.*

Getting to Yes: Methods for Achieving Consensus

Achieving consensus involves avoiding "either-or" thinking and emphasizes "both-and" thinking. Thus facilitating decision making by consensus must involve questions such as "How can we achieve the advantages of *both* alternatives?" and "What changes do we need to make so that this alternative is acceptable to you?"

Five additional methods can help you reach consensus with your team members:

1. Discussing the strengths and weaknesses of each alternative
2. Merging alternatives
3. Lobbying for an alternative
4. Conducting a cost-benefit analysis for each alternative
5. Ranking the alternatives

Discussing Strengths and Weaknesses. At this point, you will have in front of you the summaries for your alternatives, which you elaborated in Exercises 7.3 and 7.4. They list both monetary and nonmonetary benefits for each alternative. Engaging in a discussion in which you compare the strengths and weaknesses of each alternative will help the group further clarify which alternative is best. Even if you cannot agree on a solution after doing so, you will have a better understanding of the pros and cons of each solution, which will help you engage in further cross-fertilizing or merging of various alternatives.

Cross-Fertilizing and Merging Revisited. Based on the discussion of each alternative's strengths and weaknesses, you may want to boost the attractiveness of a given solution by again borrowing from other alternatives or merging it with another alternative. This is especially useful when two alternatives seem to stand out as favorites among participants. This activity allows you to create a third alternative that combines the advantages of both solutions. If you think you have already completed this step, think again. Things evolve over time, and people change their views. At this point, some participants may have a better understanding of a solution and be open to additional cross-fertilizing and merging.

Lobbying. With lobbying, one or more team members who favor a particular solution mount a compelling case for it. The idea is to capitalize on the enthusiasm, talents, and persuasive abilities of these participants. This often helps bring the group to consensus with few or no changes to a given alternative.

Cost-Benefit Analysis. Cost-benefit analysis is method of weighing the financial benefits of a particular solution against its costs over a given period of time. This analysis is often used before making a serious decision that involves large sums of money and can help you decide whether the costs involved are justified or not. If you are interested in this topic, you will want to consult one of the volumes suggested in Appendix A under "Decision Making" to find out how to conduct this analysis in a more detailed and accurate way.

Here I will provide a cost-benefit analysis for Waferinc to illustrate how it works. For each alternative, the members of the problem-solving team estimated the costs as well as the yearly financial benefits. They divided the costs into the estimated yearly benefits to determine what is called the "payback period" or "payback time." This is the time that it takes for each alternative to pay for itself and start generating financial profits. In addition, they wanted to get a better idea of the financial picture in the long run. They thus calculated the financial benefits and the net profit of each alternative over a period of three years.

Let's see how Waferinc calculated the payback period for the company's first alternative. As you recall, that alternative was to discard the new—but dysfunctional—order-tracking information system and buy another system that fit the company's needs better. Hands-on training for everyone in the organization would be included as a part of the solution. The company first estimated the costs that would be involved and then calculated the financial benefits. (It is assumed that the costs will be expended during the first year and that the benefits will accrue annually.)

Costs

New system development and installation: $40,000

Training: $5,000

Other (lost time during training, inefficiencies during the first few months, and so on): $10,000

Total costs: $55,000

Estimated Yearly Benefits

Efficiency savings throughout the company: $25,000

Improved customer service and retention: $30,000

Improved sales capability: $15,000

Total estimated yearly benefits: $70,000

Payback Period

$55,000/$70,000 = 0.78 year, or approximately 9.5 months

Table 7.1 shows the costs, benefits per year, payback period, and benefits and net profit over three years that were associated with all three alternatives that Waferinc was considering. Comparing the alternatives with respect to the payback time, alternative 2 would start to pay back the soonest, after about 6.6 months. However, looking at the total benefits over three years after subtraction of total costs (net profit), alternative 3 would provide the greatest net profit to the organization. Using this analysis, then, alternative 3 would be the best solution.

Table 7.1 Cost-Benefit Analysis for Waferinc

Alternatives	Total Costs	Benefits per Year	Payback Period	Benefits in Three Years	Net Profit in Three Years
1. Buy new system and offer training to all employees	$55,000	$70,000	9.5 months	$210,000	$155,000
2. Make system more user-friendly and offer training to all employees	$25,000	$45,000	6.6 months	$135,000	$110,000
3. Completely revamp system and offer training to all employees	$50,000	$72,000	8.3 months	$216,000	$166,000

Ranking the Alternatives

I am going to suggest here one of the simplest ways of using evaluation criteria to rank alternatives. A slew of methods have been developed in this area, and if you need more information, you can consult some of the resources listed in Appendix A under "Decision Making." The following steps, however, should suffice for your needs:

Step 1. The facilitator asks participants to come up with evaluation criteria that will be used to rank each alternative. Here are some examples:

Saves money

Is cost-effective

Increases profits

Supports competitive strategy

Builds customer loyalty

Is feasible

Can be completed on time

Step 2. The facilitator helps the team prioritize the criteria and then select three to five criteria to be used for the evaluation.

Step 3. Participants rank the solutions in each of the selected evaluation categories by using a scale from 1 to 4 as follows:

1 = solution does not meet the criterion

2 = solution partially meets the criterion

3 = solution meets the criterion

4 = solution exceeds the criterion

Step 4. The facilitator helps the team complete an evaluation grid. The alternatives are listed down the left-hand side and the evaluation criteria along the top of the grid. Each participant then scores the alternatives in each evaluation category. The facilitator writes down the individual scores and then adds the individual scores for each criterion together and divides by the number of participants in order to arrive at the mean score for that criterion. For each alternative, the facilitator then adds all of the mean criteria scores together. The alternative with the highest total score is the best choice.

Table 7.2 is a hypothetical evaluation grid for our example of Waferinc's order-tracking database system. The three alternatives are shown in the left-hand column and are evaluated by four participants against three different criteria, which are listed at the top of the grid. The boxes reveal both the individual and average scores for each alternative in each evaluation category. Total scores for each alternative are listed in the rightmost column. As you can see, alternative 3 had the highest score and was therefore the best solution based on this evaluation method.

Table 7.2 Ranking the Alternatives

		Criteria		
Alternatives	Cost-Effectiveness	Time to Complete	Maximization of Customer Benefits	Totals
1. Buy new system and offer training to all employees	1 + 2 + 1 + 1 = 5 5 ÷ 4 = 1.25	1 + 1 + 1 + 1 = 4 4 ÷ 4 = 1	3 + 3 + 3 + 3 = 12 12 ÷ 4 = 3	1.25 + 1 + 3 = 5.25
2. Make system more user-friendly and offer training to all employees	3 + 4 + 3 + 4 = 14 14 ÷ 4 = 3.5	4 + 4 + 3 + 4 = 15 15 ÷ 4 = 3.75	1 + 1 + 2 + 1 = 5 5 ÷ 4 = 1.25	3.5 + 3.75 + 4 = 8.5
3. Completely revamp system and offer training to all employees	3 + 2 + 2 + 3 = 10 10 ÷ 4 = 2.5	3 + 2 + 2 + 2 = 9 9 ÷ 4 = 2.25	4 + 4 + 4 + 4 = 16 16 ÷ 4 = 4	2.5 + 2.25 + 4 = 8.75

Making the Final Decision

No matter what method or methods you use, be they quantitative or qualitative, precise or general, remember that the bottom line is to get the team to make a decision. After you go through each method, check for consensus by asking the same questions:

- Which alternative is acceptable to you?
- What changes do we need to make so that this alternative would be acceptable to you?

What is most important for all team members during this period is the belief that they *will* be able to synthesize a solution that will lead them to consensus. And it is even more important that facilitators and team leaders hold this belief and conduct meetings in this spirit. I can still remember an awkward gathering in which both the facilitators and the leaders felt hopeless about the process and the potential for reaching a decision. As they crumbled, so did the entire group, and the meeting became a complete disaster. So be forewarned that there will be times when your situation may seem beyond help or hope. Rest assured, things do work out! Conveying this is one of the greatest contributions you can make as a team member, leader, or facilitator.

Refining the Solution

Once you have achieved consensus and have chosen your solution, you will have the opportunity to make your solution even better! I would particularly recommend this step if you achieved consensus quickly. Here are a few avenues you can follow to refine the solution:

- *Expand.* Take another pass at it by considering your previous alternatives, as well as the ideas that you did not use to create your alternatives. Your approach could be "Let's borrow! Let's incorpo-

rate as many ideas into the solution to make it as good as possible."
Also, if you can merge the solution with one or more of the other
alternatives, do so at this stage.

• *Redesign.* Spend some time redesigning your solution to account for any of its weaknesses. You may have already identified
some of these weaknesses with your team. If so, revisit them. If not,
consider what they might be. Alternatively, you can ask outsiders
to review your solution and point out weaknesses or anticipate any
negative consequences to the solution that your team did not see or
expect. Any weaknesses you come up with are likely to be minor or
to manifest themselves only a small percentage of the time, but they
are worth addressing because doing so will make your solution even
better. You should be able to account for these weaknesses without
losing the advantages of your solution.

The airline industry did this, for example, with the meal service
system it had developed on long flights. While the system provided
meal options that were satisfactory for most passengers, it had a
weakness in that it did not accommodate passengers with special
needs, such as vegetarians or people on restricted diets. Although
this weakness affected only a small percentage of passengers, airlines
redesigned the meal service system so that passengers with special
needs could order custom meals ahead of time. This greatly
enhanced customer satisfaction.

• *Test.* See if you can pilot-test your solution. This can easily
be done for training or organizational change projects, for example.
In such cases, you could offer training or implement an organizational change program, such as a new incentive scheme, with one
or two units in your company first. You could then evaluate the results and use the lessons learned to debug your solution before
extending it to the entire company.

You can also use pilot testing for a variety of other projects, such
as implementing new software programs, new products, or new
facilities designs. One way of pilot testing is to build prototypes
(small-scale models) for your solutions, which you can share with
both employees and customers for feedback.

- *Simplify.* Try to simplify the solution so that everyone can understand it. A solution that is difficult to understand is also hard to communicate and sell to others. You'll know if it is too complicated when you try to verbalize it. If you find that you cannot speak about it effectively, you suddenly feel awkward, and you get all sorts of questions and blank stares, then you know that your solution is not clear or is too complex. Test your solution by communicating it verbally to a few others as the first step toward finding out whether you need to modify it or not. Ask for feedback so that you can make it simpler and clearer.

- *Build in flexibility.* Do not forget to build flexibility into the solution. Even the best and most brilliant solutions require modifications, both as they are being implemented and soon afterward. This is why you need to craft solutions that can be adapted and changed as necessary.

For example, information technology projects tend to need changes and additional work every step of the way. Moreover, they often require that companies and vendors work cooperatively to devise user-friendly, understandable, and adaptable solutions. Therefore, you might want to build into your solution—up front—ways in which your team or organization can be in communication with the vendor to refine the project as needed. This will not only allow you to make the system more effective but will also empower your organization to continually upgrade the system in the future.

The design of new products or new product features also requires considerable flexibility. This, of course, is a vast topic on which volumes have been written. Briefly, however, I can say that when it comes to design projects, it is important to divorce yourselves from expectations about the final product. This means that you and your team need to be open to required changes during the implementation process. Your organization may, for example, decide that it needs to eliminate some exciting yet expensive design feature to make a new product more affordable. Staying open to these modifications can be critical for ensuring the product's ultimate success.

Think also about providing flexibility for your end users. For instance, installing an information system that creates a predetermined number and type of reports may not be the best solution because it will limit your users greatly. You might instead want to devise a system that allows users the flexibility, say, to design their own reports.

If appropriate to your particular situation, you might want to think about designing solutions that are modular. Car manufacturers, for example, are increasingly building cars using modular designs in which the same car engines and chassis can be used to construct a variety of different models. Such design modularity also provides flexibility for buyers in choosing features such as seats, sound systems, design features, and even engines. Modularity has also been applied to the design of personal computers. So try to think of your solution in modular terms where applicable and whenever possible.

Finally, in considering issues of flexibility, think about the future. For example, think about what you might need to provide your users so that they can continue to improve your solution in the future. If you are designing an employee coaching system, for instance, you might want to enlarge your solution by providing employees with additional resources for further skill and career development.

The solution-refining process can potentially go on forever. Be sure to set up a deadline by which you will complete any modifications to the solution and move toward action planning and implementation. The next chapter will discuss this final step of the problem-solving process.

Points to Remember

- To develop a number of different solution options, team members first prioritize all of the ideas they brainstormed and then group them into alternatives.

- To turn alternatives into fully operational solutions, you may cross-fertilize them to incorporate ideas from one into another; merge two alternatives to create a third, better option; and add further details.

- The solution your team finally selects will be the most successful if you arrive at it through consensus. This means that all team members understand the selected alternative, can live with it, and will support it.

- You can undertake additional activities to achieve consensus, including discussing alternatives' strengths and weaknesses, merging alternatives, lobbying for a particular alternative, applying cost-benefit analysis, and ranking alternatives.

- Once you have chosen a solution, you can further refine it by incorporating unused ideas into it, remedying any of its weaknesses, pilot-testing it, simplifying it, and building flexibility into it.

Chapter Eight

Taking Action

Whatever you can, or dream you can, begin it.
Boldness has genius, power, and magic in it.
—Johann Wolfgang von Goethe

By this point, you have a healthy and robust solution in front of you that addresses the problem that you identified in Chapter One and perhaps even goes beyond it. It's now time to take the plunge and turn that solution into a reality!

What you need at this stage is a step-by-step action plan that will systematically move you from where you are now to where you want to be in the future. This chapter will help you design a plan that includes both short- and long-term action items. It will lead you in thinking about the most risky aspects of your plan and help you design avenues to overcome them or work around them. In addition, it will give you the opportunity to develop a strategy for communicating your chosen alternative throughout your organization, and it will provide you with a blueprint for transitioning to your new solution. Finally, it will teach you how to evaluate your implementation efforts and make future improvements to your solution.

Readiness for Action

As I have observed in my work with clients, the main stumbling block at this point in the process is fear, which is generally manifested as resistance to change. I have seen organizations hesitate to take a leap either because they were afraid that the solution would fail or because they feared the disruption involved in implementing the changes that the solution would require. Wouldn't it be pitiful if the destiny of your innovative solution were a dusty shelf?

To help you avoid such a scenario, I encourage you to recall from Chapter Two the discussion about why people resist change. As you may remember, we resist change in the following circumstances:

- When we don't have a clear picture of what it involves or will lead to
- When it is imposed on us
- When it means that we will lose something of benefit to us
- When it interferes with our current priorities

By now, these considerations should have been largely overcome within your team through the process of developing the solution by following the methods featured throughout this book. As you have experienced firsthand, your solution is the outcome of a common vision, everyone's ideas, and consensus decision making. Every member of your team understands, supports, and can live with the solution that you came up with for your project. Moreover, this process of developing solutions fuels team members with enthusiasm and commitment, which are necessary during this final stage of action planning and implementation.

The exercises in this chapter are designed to dispel any last concerns that may be lingering in the minds of team members and, even more importantly, to help you preempt any fears about the change effort that may arise in your organization. These exercises guide you to create an action plan so that everyone affected by the change has a crystal-clear picture of what it involves. The exercises will help you communicate your solution to the rest of the organization in a positive way that is designed to generate acceptance and commitment.

What might also help your team at this stage is to review the discussions in Chapter Two attesting to the fact that most of our worst fears never actually materialize and that the only way to deal with them is by taking action. Furthermore, I encourage you to seek inspiration in positive thinking and in your connection with your Higher Power. Assuming that you believe in such a Higher Power, you can rest assured that it will provide you with all the help and resources you need to move forward. You really don't have to go it alone!

The following exercise further reinforces your team's readiness for action.

Exercise 8.1: Readiness for Action

Step 1: Reexamine the Solution

Have your team take a careful look at your solution and then ponder or even meditate on the following questions. In answering these questions, everyone should be instructed to focus on the response that comes from the gut, not the head.

- Does your solution advance your vision for the problem?
- Is your solution broad enough to replace the problem with opportunity?
- Would implementing the solution lead to many positive results for you, your work environment, and the people around you?

If you find that the intuitive, instinctive reaction on the part of project owners and most team members is yes, you are ready for action. Proceed with the next two steps. They will further fortify the team with positive thinking and readiness for action. Moreover, they will motivate even those members who may feel uneasy at this point.

Step 2: Anticipate Positive Results

As a next step, have each team member list all the advantages and positive results that your solution is expected to achieve.

Step 3: Consider Missed Opportunities

Have your team consider what opportunities would be missed by not going ahead with this solution.

Step 4: Examine the Solution One Last Time

Repeat the questions that you asked in step 1. What answers are you getting from your team members at this point?

If there are still quite a few team members who feel uneasy, explain to them that the final step of the methodology, taking action, is designed to make the solution as doable as possible.

Designing Your Action Plan

Having completed Exercise 8.1, you and your team have cemented your enthusiasm for moving ahead with your solution. You are now ready to get down to the nuts and bolts of devising an action plan. This is largely a practical, left-brain activity. It relies on the pragmatism of sensing types rather than the creativity of intuitive types. This does not mean, of course, that intuitive types should not be involved in the process. Your action plan must still be creative in order to mobilize your resources in the most effective way, but the balance is now seriously tipping toward practicality and feasibility.

Planning is, of course, the main engine that drives every project. Some of you may see planning as a tedious activity, but you will tackle it by following the steps of this section. I will guide you to do the following:

- Start thinking about the three basic dimensions of any plan: scope, time, and resources
- Devise both a long-range and short-term plan
- Set up contingency plans to minimize risks

Scope, Time, and Resources

The first task in designing your plan is to ask questions regarding the three most critical dimensions of any project: scope, time, and resources. *Scope* refers to the overall extent of your project—the range of activities that your solution will involve. In considering questions about scope, you may decide that you want to implement your solution in major phases or parts rather than all at once. This can help you break your solution down into chunks that are more doable.

For instance, let's return to Chapter Seven's example of a project seeking to build excellence in supervision through training and support services. A team considering such an undertaking might want to separate this kind of project into four phases. The first phase would involve identifying available resources such as training and supervisor support programs. The second phase would involve interviewing individuals and groups within the organization for the purpose of identifying what your training needs are. During the third phase, the team would decide which training and support programs best meet those needs. And during the fourth phase, the organization would actually implement the training and support programs.

The other two important dimensions to consider for any project are time and resources. *Time* refers to how long you will need—or, sometimes more importantly, how long you *have*—to complete the implementation of your entire solution. *Resources* are the information, knowledge, funds, people, and equipment you'll need in order to make your solution a reality.

Exercise 8.2: Clarifying Scope, Time, and Resources

As a team, work on the following questions.

Scope

Think about the scope of your project, the range of activities that your solution will require. List them one by one.

Do you want to tackle the solution in its entirety, or would you prefer to separate it into phases or parts?

Which phases can you identify right now?

Time

What is your timeline for implementing the solution?

Resources

What types of resources (funds, information, knowledge, people, and equipment) are needed to complete the solution?

Which of those resources are available within your organization? Where are they available?

Which resources are not available within your organization?

How might you go about obtaining such resources?

The Action Plan

Now that you have defined the scope, timeline, and resources you'll need for your solution, you have the overall parameters of a step-by-step action plan. Although the creation of an action plan can be something that one person can take on as a solo project, I recommend that you do it working with your team, as you have throughout most of this book. You can, of course, assign some tasks to different individuals and subgroups in order to speed up the process. But you will then still meet as a team to refine and finalize your work collectively. Again, you may want at this stage to consider expanding your group with pragmatic sensing types who have relevant expertise and experience.

It is also imperative that you continue to have your planning meetings facilitated. This will allow you to maximize your time together and meet your objectives in the most effective way. As always, the facilitator can be an external consultant or someone from inside the organization who will not be affected by the action plan. Please be sure to set an agenda, clear objectives, and ground rules and success criteria for your planning meetings. Also ensure effective scribing for each of your meetings. (For a refresher on these elements, see Chapter Four.)

The worksheet in Exercise 8.3 provides the blueprint for building the action plan. It uses a two-stage approach. During the first stage, you take a long-term view of your project and develop an action plan for all of the different phases of your solution. During the second stage, you complete a short-term plan. The short-term plan consists of all of the tasks that you and your team, working together or individually, can accomplish immediately. This will allow you to identify tasks that you can complete fairly easily and quickly so that you can get moving on the project right away.

Once your team or organization has accomplished the activities of the first short-term plan, I recommend that you create a new short-term plan for the next series of activities. This will continue to occur until you work yourselves all the way through the various phases of your long-term plan. The process will keep you and your team focused and excited. After all, every major work is completed a day at a time. Before you know it, the time will pass and your solution will be implemented!

Completing the action plan worksheets consists of providing answers to the following open-ended questions:

1. *What steps* need to be completed during each phase of your project?

2. *Who* will complete each step?

3. *When* will each step be started and completed?

4. *How* will each step be completed?

Exercise 8.3: Creating Action Plan Worksheets

With your team, take some time to think of all the steps that will be required to complete your entire project (long-term plan). On flipchart paper, create a worksheet like the one shown here. On it, list all of the steps in sequence. Then, for each step, write down answers to the following questions:

- Who will be involved in completing this step?

- When will this step start and when will it finish?

- How will this step be completed?

After completing the long-term plan, think about the steps that you can complete immediately (short-term plan). List them in sequence, and again answer the questions about who, when, and how for each step.

I also recommend that you assign a team member or the minute taker to record your work on the worksheets. You can then distribute your plan to all team members.

Action Plan Worksheet

Long-Term Plan			
Step	Who	When (Start and End Dates)	How

Short-Term Plan (immediate action steps)			
Step	Who	When (Start and End Dates)	How

Southwestern Clinic's Action Plan for Excellence in Patient Satisfaction

Southwestern Clinic is a nonprofit organization that provides health care services and education to its community. Although the clinic was doing a superb job of delivering quality health care, patient satisfaction with customer service consistently suffered. The team of top executives at Southwestern Clinic decided to take action. They defined their vision in one sentence: we achieve excellence in patient care throughout the organization. They agreed that their first project would be to improve customer service. Moreover, they developed a specific objective: to improve the patient satisfaction index by 30 percent within one year after the completion of the project.

The director of human resources (HR) was asked by the clinic's president to lead the design of the project. The executive team, which in this case was the project team as well, met numerous times and determined that the best solution alternative was as follows:

1. To enhance the customer service skills of employees through training

2. To make certain that these new skills were transferred to the workplace and translated into higher patient satisfaction by creating employee support systems that reinforced the needed behaviors

3. To use an outside vendor to design and deliver the training and develop employee support systems

4. To bring in an outside facilitator to conduct one-on-one and group interviews to help employees identify and prioritize the clinic's needs and provide support during crucial meetings

Once they had developed the solution, the team of executives met several times to design the action plan. Their plan, with its long- and short-term components, is illustrated in Exhibit 8.1.

Minimizing Risks

By embarking on your action plan, you have decided to take the leap because you know that your solution is right for you and the people around you. Yet this does not mean that you have to leap in the dark. You can identify potential risks that might be associated with your plan and think of ways to minimize or work around them.

Some of these aspects might be related to the unavailability or overcommitment of certain resources (such as funds, information, knowledge, technology, or people). Perhaps some key people may not be fully dedicated to the project, for instance. Or you may be embarking on tasks that are using new technologies, which may present risks. Other risks relate to overoptimistic or very tight deadlines. Yet others may have to do with the nature of certain action steps.

Exhibit 8.1 Southwestern Clinic's Action Plan

Long-Term Plan

Step	Who	When (Start and End Dates)	How
Reworking of action plan in partnership with vendor	Team and vendor	Next 2 months	Meeting
Interviews	Facilitator	Month 3	One on one and group meetings
Training program design	Vendor	Month 3	Customize program to meet identified needs
Support systems design	Vendor	Month 3	Customize offerings to meet identified needs
Finalization of training and support systems	Facilitator, vendor, and team	Month 3	Facilitated problem-solving session
Identification and recruitment of trainees	Operations and HR directors	Month 4	Talk to unit managers
Pretraining skills assessment	Vendor	Month 4	Use a skills test
Training	Vendor	Months 4–8	Training sessions in the clinic conference room
Support systems launch	Vendor, HR director, and team	Month 4	Vendor to do it in partnership with HR
Progress evaluation and adjustments	Facilitator, vendor, and team	Month 6	Facilitated problem-solving session

Posttraining skills assessment	Vendor	Month 8	Use skills test
Comparison of patient satisfaction index levels prior to and after the completion of the program	Vendor and operations director	End of year	Summarize monthly survey data with baseline satisfaction levels
Progress evaluation and adjustments	Facilitator, vendor, and team	End of year	Facilitated problem-solving session

Short-Term Plan (immediate action steps)

Step	Who	When (*Start and End Dates*)	How
Consultation with other clinics	HR director	Today and tomorrow	Contact association of clinics and discuss with other HR directors with similar experiences
Development of request for proprosals	HR director and team	End of this week	Follow examples of previous requests for proposals
Identification of vendors	HR director	End of this month	Talk to training and development associations; get referrals from other clinics
Selection of vendor	Team	End of month 2	Make decisions preferably by consensus
Baseline for patient satisfaction performance	Operations director	End of this month	Summarize this month's patient surveys

You can brainstorm with your team about what some of the risks associated with your plan might be and then prioritize them according to their seriousness. Southwestern Clinic, for example, identified the risk that heavy workloads might result in low participation in the new training program. The members of the executive team therefore brainstormed and decided to offer the training program in three-hour chunks on Friday mornings, which traditionally have lower patient volumes. Exercise 8.4 guides you to discuss and prioritize the riskiest aspects of your project and then find ways for overcoming each one.

Exercise 8.4: Minimizing Your Risks

1. Prepare a chart with two columns on flipchart paper. Head the first column "Top Risks" and the second column "Alternative Actions."

   Top Risks   *Alternative Actions*

2. The facilitator asks your team, "What serious risks can you anticipate regarding the various aspects of your plan, in terms of scheduling and time needed, resources, and the various steps involved?" Next, the facilitator guides everyone in prioritizing the risks according to their level of seriousness. The most serious risks are recorded in the left-hand column of the chart.

3. Then the team thinks of alternative ways to overcome each risk by asking the following questions:

- How can we prevent this risk?
- How can we overcome or minimize this factor?
- What are some alternative ways of accomplishing this difficult step?

Record the answers in the right-hand column of the chart.

Other Aspects of Your Action Plan

We will now work on four other necessary aspects of your plan (see Figure 8.1):

1. Communicating the solution
2. Managing the transition
3. Evaluating the solution
4. Planning future improvements

Communicating the Solution

Communicating the solution is a critical step because it provides others in the organization with the information they need in order to understand what the project will entail. Providing appropriate

Figure 8.1 Special Considerations for Your Action Plan

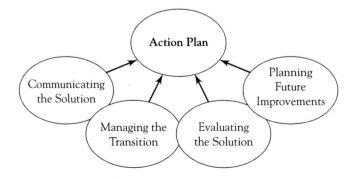

information is necessary to ease people's fears about change. Effective communication allows you, your team, and your organization to avoid confusion, unclear expectations, rumors, and resistance.

Communicating the solution effectively is also crucial because it allows you to spread your enthusiasm about the coming change. It offers you the chance to assure everyone that the proposed solution will work out and lead to improvements.

Earlier, you had the opportunity to run your project by several outsiders in order to test it and improve it. What you will do now is put together an even simpler presentation describing the solution and some details of the action plan. You will then devise a communication strategy for bringing it to the rest of your organization.

A good communication strategy provides a vehicle for clarification and ongoing dialogue during the implementation stage. The objectives of your strategy are twofold: to identify champions for communicating the selected alternative and to broadcast the solution to everyone who needs to understand it and endorse it because it will affect them directly or indirectly.

To create your strategy, you can take the following steps:

1. Determine who needs to be informed about the solution and the action plan.

2. Identify who among your team members can serve as your communication champions. The best candidates would ideally be those who like to interact with other people (extroverts) and who are articulate presenters.

3. Identify the avenues that you can use to deliver the presentation, such as open meetings, internal communication letters, and intranet messages from communications champions.

4. Call an open forum to present the solution and action plan and to answer any questions people may have.

5. Have your champions communicate the solutions specifically to the various divisions, departments, and units that will be

affected directly or indirectly by the change. These champions will address the questions and concerns of individuals who did not attend the open forum. In addition, they can serve as direct points of contact for these divisions, departments, and units during implementation.

6. Create an ongoing discussion forum (either online or through a physical message board at some central location such as a cafeteria) that informs people about the latest developments and provides an open channel of communication.

The next exercise guides you in formulating a communication strategy.

Exercise 8.5: Communicating the Solution

As a team, write down answers to the following questions:

Who needs to be informed about your solution?

Which team members would like to serve as communication champions?

How will you communicate the solution?

What venue will you use as an open channel of communication during implementation?

What steps do you need to add to your action plan in order to factor in the aspect of communicating the solution?

Managing the Transition

With problem solving, it's easy to take the present reality, place it next to the future picture of reality promised by your solution, and think that only these two realities exist. Don't forget, however, that getting from here to there, from your present situation to your future situation, means you'll need to go through a period of transition (see Figure 8.2). You need to get through all of that time in which the old is being replaced with the new. In order for this transition to happen successfully, you must carefully plan and manage it.

Richard Beckhard and Reuben Harris, organizational change experts, point out the need for creating special managerial roles and structures in order to make effective organizational transitions. This may include appointing one or more people who have the authority and power to mobilize resources to oversee the transition. Such managerial roles and structures may take different forms, including these:

- A special chief executive named to direct the entire effort
- A project manager charged with coordinating the transition
- A natural leader designated to manage the transition who is trusted by employees who will be most affected by the transition
- An advisory committee or group of individuals representing various functions that may be affected by the change

At Southwestern Clinic, for example, the transition management structure consisted of a cross-sectional committee of individuals

Figure 8.2 Transitioning

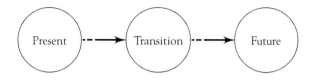

from various units of the organization. Although the human resource director led the design of the project, the group unanimously selected the director of operations as the head of the transitioning effort—not only because he was a natural leader but also because he had direct authority over the various unit managers at the clinic, control of the budget, and responsibility for overseeing day-to-day operations.

Managing a transition effectively means that your organization will maintain the same level of performance and customer service throughout the change period. You may, for example, be engaged in a major organizational change that includes training hundreds of employees from different shifts. Such a project requires careful consideration of how you will maintain the required levels of production and customer service while the trainees are away from the shop floor.

Or you may be involved in a project to install new automated equipment that will increase productivity and efficiency. It usually takes a few weeks to a few months before everyone knows how to work the new system without downtime. Managing the transition in this case requires that you plan how to maintain your production levels while the new automated system is being debugged. For many organizations, this requires keeping old equipment running in parallel with new systems for a period of time.

The next exercise supports you in planning and managing the transition.

Exercise 8.6: Planning the Transition

Have your team meet to answer the following questions, and modify your action plan accordingly.

Which individual or individuals will manage the transition?

What steps must you take to keep your levels of performance the same during the transition?

Who can assist you in accomplishing these steps?

When do you need to take these steps?

How can the steps be completed in the most effective manner?

What modifications or additions must you make to your action plan in order to accommodate these steps?

Evaluating the Solution

From Edwards Deming to Gerald Nadler, experts have long advocated the importance of evaluation in achieving excellence. That means that as you begin to take the steps outlined in your action plan, you will periodically need to assess whether you are achieving the results that you expected. It also means you'll need to take stock of your solution as a whole after it has been institutionalized. This will allow you to identify what needs to be improved so that you can continue to advance toward your vision. Moreover, it will also let you see what needs to be celebrated and what lessons you have learned.

Program evaluation is often a complex process and cannot be an afterthought. It must be integrated into your action plan. This is because it involves collecting and summarizing data, which can be a complicated and expensive process. I recommend that you base your evaluation on your project's quantifiable objective(s), which you developed in Chapter Six.

For example, as you will recall, Southwestern Clinic's objective was to improve the patient satisfaction index by 30 percent within one year after completion of the project. The clinic's executives decided to track this using customer service surveys. They accessed the data from their existing customer service survey to establish baseline patient satisfaction levels prior to starting the program. They then collected and summarized patient survey data on a monthly basis as they were implementing their solution, but they did not make any comparisons until the program was completed.

Another effective and quick way to evaluate your solution is to conduct internal group interviews, which will be explained later in the chapter. The purpose of these interviews is to discuss progress and identify areas for improvement.

Exercise 8.7 will help you integrate program evaluation into your action plan. Exercise 8.8 will then give you more specifics on how to conduct the evaluation both during and after the transition.

Exercise 8.7: Working Program Evaluation into Your Action Plan

With your team, answer the following questions:

How often do you plan to evaluate your efforts?

When do you plan to conduct a final evaluation of your solution?

Have you obtained baseline data for the quantifiable objective(s) of your project?

How do you plan to gather that data for program evaluation?

Who is responsible for completing the evaluations?

How do you need to modify your action plan to include the evaluation process?

Exercise 8.8: Evaluating Your Implementation Efforts

At the completion of each phase of your project and at the conclusion of your project as a whole, set aside some time with your team to answer the following questions:

How well are we performing against the action plan?

How well are we performing against the scope, timeline, and resources of the project?

What successes have we experienced?

What failures have we encountered?

Do we need to make changes to our action plan?

Planning Future Improvements

No solution is ever final. New developments are bound to arise, and changes will be necessary at some point. You need to keep your solution flexible and open to improvements, even once you think you are through with it.

If you design a software project, for instance, you'll need to build it as an open system that others can understand, work with, modify, and expand in the future. And be aware that evaluation and future improvements go hand in hand. You can think of each evaluation milestone as an opportunity for improving your solution. Even once your solution is completely implemented, it is useful to continue evaluating, motivating change, building new solutions, and improving the situation over and over again.

For example, Southwestern Clinic considered pursuing improvements six months after completing the customer service program. While the clinic did achieve higher patient satisfaction levels based on its customer surveys, the executives decided to do more. They conducted a facilitated group interview with fifteen employees and managers from various units. The group members discussed the positive effects of the program and how to improve it. As next steps, they decided to revamp their incentive schemes in order to achieve even better customer service levels. Moreover, they decided to follow up with a supervisory skills program for unit managers.

Exercise 8.9 helps you plan for future improvements; Exercise 8.10 then guides you to consider future improvements for your solution.

Exercise 8.9: Planning Future Improvements

With your team, answer the following questions:

At what point will you consider brainstorming about improving your solution?

Do you need to modify your action plan to take this future activity into account?

Exercise 8.10: Future Improvements

Make two columns on a sheet of flipchart paper. Head the first column "Successes to Date" and the second column "Possible Improvements."

Successes to Date	*Possible Improvements*

Conduct a brainstorming session to plan for improvements to your solution. Ask the following questions:

- What successes have you had to this point?
- How can we make our solution even better?

Record the answers in the appropriate columns on the chart.

Taking the Plunge

You now have both your solution and your action plan. In addition to giving you a step-by-step road map for implementing your project, your plan allows you to communicate the solution, manage the transition, evaluate your progress, make future improvements, and minimize risks.

As Aristotle said, "Well begun is half done." You're now well past the beginning part of the solution path, which means that you're more than halfway there!

What you need at this point are perseverance and the ability to remain flexible. Remember that even the best solutions sometimes need to be altered and changed. Life has a way of showing us where we can and cannot go. The general conditions of the economy may evolve for better or worse. Or as you see the first results of your solution, you may realize that you need to make some adjustments. Just keep in mind that change and the need for change are natural occurrences that continue to happen over time. So stay open to all possibilities and opportunities!

The leaders of an engineering research and development firm, for example, dreamed of creating the best radar solutions for defense applications. They successfully secured federal grants to design these applications and transfer them to the Department of Defense (DoD). They thought they had a done deal and earnestly went to work on their project. Then, the DoD did not fund their projects and their dreams started to evaporate. After spending three years designing several applications, they were able to transfer only one of them to the DoD.

Despite this devastating blow, the firm was able to stay flexible enough to reroute its course in midstream. Realizing that their original plans would not materialize, the executives decided to apply the firm's technology to commercial applications. In fact, they were able to obtain additional federal funds to do so in a number of fields, including transportation and underwater mapping. They successfully sold their new applications—and lo and behold, defense budgets began to increase again, and they were able to pursue new plans to develop applications for the DoD. Flexibility and continuous action were the keys to this company's success.

So as you embark on your action plan, remember the many ways you learned about in this book for staying positive. Remember that things generally turn out fine. If a situation becomes difficult, you can always make use of your Positive Action Toolbox by taking your Positive Inventory, visualizing, praying, meditating, and so forth. And remember that your team, your personal and professional allies, and your Higher Power are always there to provide you with support. So go ahead and take the plunge!

Points to Remember

- Developing the action plan starts with considering the steps involved in its different phases (*scope*), the *timeline* for completing these phases, and the *resources* you will need in terms of funds, information, knowledge, people, and equipment.

- It is helpful to include practical sensing types on your team for the nuts-and-bolts activity of action planning.

- Formulating an action plan includes plotting out short- and long-term activities and goals.

- Action planning also involves identifying and reducing risks, communicating the solution, managing the transition, evaluating the solution, and planning for future improvements.

- No matter what, things always turn out fine.

Conclusion

Looking Toward the Future

If you have arrived at this part of *The Solution Path*, you are well on your way to completing your project and turning your current challenge into an opportunity. Congratulations!

Depending on the solution you have developed, however, you may be addressing only a piece of the vision, the self-fulfilling prophecy that you developed for your challenge. As you will recall, you generated a portfolio of projects about how to achieve your vision in Chapter Six. You chose to work on a feasible first project, which solves your original problem, promises maximum results, and gets you closer to your vision. You then created numerous ideas and turned them into solution alternatives. Finally, you embarked on one particular solution that promised to accomplish your goals. Keep in mind that the rest of your projects may also be formulated into further solutions that can keep you chipping away at different aspects of your vision. So go back, prioritize them, pick one, and use this book to guide you once more as you carry out each new project.

Whether you are addressing some or all of your vision, there is always more work to be done. You can keep refining your efforts on this one particular problem, or you can begin to address other challenges. Life and work constantly provide us with opportunities for growth. I hope that this book has inspired you to see this process as an exciting one that will charge you with energy.

Raised on the classics, I always found inspiration in the *Odyssey*, an epic story written by Homer more than twenty-five hundred years ago. The book's hero, Odysseus, was one of the leaders of the Trojan War. Because of the destruction he wreaked on the city of Troy, he was condemned by the gods to wander over the sea for many years while he continued his efforts to return to Ithaca, his small island kingdom. Despite this exhausting journey, Odysseus ultimately achieved his goal and succeeded in returning home to Ithaca.

Although Odysseus's persistence, creativity, and passion inspired me, I was always perplexed as to why he had to solve so many difficult problems in order to achieve his vision. It was not until I read a poem by C. P. Cavafy titled "Ithaca" that I was finally able to reconcile my feelings. In the poem, Cavafy emphasizes that the process rather than the ultimate outcome is really what matters most, because this is how we gain knowledge and experience. He ends "Ithaca" with these lines:

> *And even if you find her poor, Ithaca has not deceived you.*
> *As wise as you have become, so experienced,*
> *You must realize the meaning of Ithacas.*

My hope is that you, too, will realize the meaning of the many Ithacas you will be seeking in the course of your professional life. May this book serve as a companion and guide to help bring you the riches of knowledge and experience as you proceed on your path to creative and satisfying solutions.

Appendix A:
Resources

You may find the following resources helpful in expanding your understanding of various aspects of the Solution Path.

Positive Thinking

From Fear to Positive Thinking

Jeffers, S. *Feel the Fear and Do It Anyway*. New York: Fawcett, 1987.
Murphy, J. *The Power of Your Subconscious Mind*. New York: Bantam Books, 1982. (Originally published 1963)
Peale, N. *You Can If You Think You Can*. New York: Fawcett, 1974.
Ventrella, S. *The Power of Positive Thinking in Business*. New York: Fireside, 2001.

Affirmations

Frankhauser, J. *The Power of Affirmations*. Farmingdale, N.Y.: Coleman Graphics, n.d.

Positive-Oriented Books

Bach, R. *Jonathan Livingston Seagull*. Old Tappan, N.J.: Macmillan, 1970.
Fotinos, J. and Gold, A., *The Think and Grow Rich Workbook*. New York: Tarcher, 2009.
Hendricks, G., and Ludeman, K. *The Corporate Mystic*. New York: Bantam, 1996.
Hill, N., and Stone, C. *Success Through a Positive Mental Attitude*. New York: Pocket Books, 1960.
Mandino, O. *The Greatest Miracle in the World*. New York: Bantam, 1975.
Taylor, S. L. *The Opportunity in Every Problem*. Veyo, Utah: Good Samaritan, 2001.
Yogananda, P. *Inner Peace*. Los Angeles: Self-Realization Fellowship, 1999.

Working with Individuals and Teams

Personality Traits and Teams

Benfari, R. *Understanding and Changing Your Management Style*. San Francisco: Jossey-Bass, 1999.

Keirsey, D., and Bates, M. *Please Understand Me*. Del Mar, Calif.: Prometheus Nemesis, 1978.

Katzenbach, J. R., and Smith, D. K. *The Wisdom of Teams*. Boston: Harvard Business School Press, 1993.

Parker, G. M. *Cross-Functional Teams: Working with Allies, Enemies, and Other Strangers*. (2nd ed.) San Francisco: Jossey-Bass, 2002.

Riso, D and Hudson, R., *The Wisdom of the Enneagram*. New York: Bantam Books, 1999.

Scholtes, P., Joiner, B., and Streibel, B. *The Team Handbook*. (2nd ed.) Madison, Wis.: Oriel, 1996.

MBTI Personality Testing

Web sites offering testing:
> http://www.cpp-dp.com
> http://www.capt.org.

Group Facilitation

Bens, I. *Facilitating with Ease!* San Francisco: Jossey-Bass, 2000.

Doyle, M., and Straus, D. *How to Make Meetings Work*. New York: Jove Books, 1982.

Kaner, S., and others. *Facilitator's Guide to Participatory Decision-Making*. Philadelphia: New Society Publishers, 1996.

Schuman, S. (ed.), *Creating a Culture of Collaboration*. The International Association of Facilitators Handbook, San Francisco: Jossey-Bass, 2006.

Visualization

Gawain, S. *Creative Visualization*. Mill Valley, Calif.: Whatever Publishing, 1978.

Gawain, S. *Creative Visualization Meditations*. New World Library Audio, 2002.

Hall, L. "Can You Picture That?" *Training and Development Journal*, September 1990, pp. 79–81.

Schwartz, A. *Guided Imagery for Groups*. Chicago: Sterns Books, 1997

Creating Ideas and Solutions

De Bono, E. *Serious Creativity*. New York: HarperBusiness, 1992.

Gordon, J. *Synectics*. New York: HarperCollins, 1961.

Sternberg, R. (ed.) *Handbook of Creativity*. New York: Cambridge University Press, 1999.

Von Oech, R. *A Whack on the Side of the Head*. New York: Warner Books, 1983.

Decision Making

Brealey, R., and Myers, S. *Principles of Corporate Finance*. New York: McGraw-Hill, 2000.

Robbins, S., and De Cenzo, D. *Fundamentals of Management*. (2nd ed.) Upper Saddle River, N.J.: Prentice Hall, 1998.

Skinner, D. C. *Introduction to Decision Analysis: A Practitioner's Guide to Improving Decision Quality*. (2nd ed.) Gainesville, Fla.: Probabilistic Publishing, 1999.

Taking Action

Fuller, J. *Managing Performance Improvement Projects*. San Francisco: Jossey-Bass/Pfeiffer, 1997.

Hertz, D., and Thomas, H. *Risk Analysis and Its Applications*. New York: Wiley, 1983.

Lewis, J. *The Project Manager's Desk Reference*. Chicago: Probus, 1993.

Appendix B:
Your Personality Type

There are nine pairs of preferences under each one of the four personality dimensions. For each pair of preferences, choose the answer that feels most comfortable to you because that is what you do, not what you should or would like to do. Do not overanalyze; go with your "gut."

A. Extroversion or Introversion

Extroversion	Check	Introversion	Check
1 I love being with others.		I prefer solitude.	
2 In gatherings, I am excited to meet as many people as possible.		In gatherings, I interact with a few individuals.	
3 I tolerate noise.		I seek quiet.	
4 After a crowded party, I feel energized.		After a crowded party, I feel exhausted.	
5 Being alone is a chore.		Time alone fills me with energy.	
6 I love to talk to others.		I prefer to listen.	
7 I make friends everywhere.		I have a few close friends.	
8 I think out loud.		I think carefully before communicating.	
9 I prefer working with lots of people.		I prefer to concentrate on my own work.	
Total number of checks		Total number of checks	

B. Sensing or Intuiting

Sensing	Check	Intuiting	Check
1 It is most important to know the facts about a situation.		I focus on the possibilities of a situation.	
2 I am practical.		I am innovative.	
3 I focus on the present, on what is.		I look to the future, to what could be.	
4 I understand with my five senses.		My five senses are a start, but I also rely on my sixth sense.	
5 I prefer proven theories.		I love new concepts.	
6 I rely on past experience.		I rely on intuition.	
7 I use realism and common sense.		I prefer using my imagination.	
8 I prefer using hard-core data.		I prefer to think metaphorically.	
9 I am drawn to details.		I focus on the big picture.	
Total number of checks		Total number of checks	

C. Thinking or Feeling

Thinking	Check	Feeling	Check
1 I am fair and objective.		I tend to be sympathetic to others.	
2 I make decisions with my head.		I make decisions with my heart.	
3 I stay unbiased.		I am compassionate.	
4 I analyze the pros and cons of each option.		I think of how each option will affect people.	
5 I am interested in what needs to be done.		I take into account how people feel.	
6 I am logical and analytical.		I am value-oriented.	
7 I choose truth over mercy.		I choose mercy over truth.	
8 I am all for justice.		I prefer sympathy.	
9 Decisions need to be made impersonally.		Decisions need to take personal feelings into account.	
Total number of checks		Total number of checks	

D. Judging or Perceiving

Judging	Check	Perceiving	Check
1 I plan diligently.		I go with the flow.	
2 I feel better after decisions are made.		I feel better before decisions are made.	
3 I am scheduled and organized.		I am spontaneous and flexible.	
4 I hate last-minute surprises.		I love surprises.	
5 Deadlines are set in stone.		Deadlines can be changed.	
6 I take control.		I let things happen.	
7 Decisions are final.		The best decisions can be easily modified.	
8 I love punctuality.		I prefer to be leisurely.	
9 I am bothered when things are unsettled and incomplete.		I prefer it when my options are open.	
Total number of checks		Total number of checks	

After tallying the number of responses (checks) for each dimension, fill out the worksheet below. Then write in the type that received the largest number of responses on each dimension. This is your preferred style.

Dimension	Number of Checks	Number of Checks	My Type
A	Extroversion _____	Introversion _____	_____
B	Sensing _____	Intuiting _____	_____
C	Thinking _____	Feeling _____	_____
D	Judging _____	Perceiving _____	_____

Should the number of checks be split pretty evenly between the two styles of a personality dimension (say, four against five checks), this means that while you do have a preferred mode of operation, you are balanced among both types and may vary your style according to the situation.

Appendix C:
Visualization in Teams

Conducting visualizations with teams and allowing members to share their insights afterward can be an extremely powerful way of helping the group think "outside the box." The following exercise helps your team members use visualization to develop creative ideas for their vision statement. It is based on an exercise I use regularly in my seminars and classes with great success.

Visualizing with Your Team

1. Have team members divide up into pairs and discuss the problem.

2. Play gentle, soothing music in the background.

3. Have someone guide team members by reading the following visualization aloud slowly, allowing for appropriate pauses:

"Sit comfortably in your chair. Relax. Now let your eyes wander about the room and out the window. Keep letting your eyes wander.

"Now close your eyes. Let your forehead muscles loosen up, your mouth, your cheeks. Let your neck relax. Release any tension in your shoulders, your arms, and your hands, down to your palms. Drop your shoulders just a bit and let your back release. Check your legs, your knees, and your feet for tension. Just gently let it go. You are calm. Peaceful. Relaxed.

"Imagine yourself on your favorite beach. The water is so blue, so magical, so warm, so relaxing. You can hear the sound of the waves as they crash in front of your feet. So nice, so warm, so soothing.

"You're now starting to walk toward a hammock. It is nestled among the trees in front of the beach. Get into the hammock and allow yourself to get lost as you gently sway back and forth, back and forth. So relaxing.

"You suddenly see in front of you somebody who can give you all the insight you need to turn your problem around. Say to this person, 'Give me the keys to greatness.'

"Pause, look, and listen. . . . Stay still, see, and listen.

"What is this person saying to you?

"What are you doing?

"What are you supposed to be doing?

"How are others behaving?

"What ideas are coming to you?

"Now slowly come back into the room, and gently open your eyes."

4. Have the partners write down answers to the following questions:

   Do you have any new insights about the problem?

   Can you feel or sense any new or compelling directions for the vision statement?

5. Have the partners share their insights with one another. Then have them report to the larger team.

6. Ask individuals to write down all the new ideas that have come to them as a result of this process.

Bibliography

Beckhard, R., and Harris, R. *Organizational Transitions: Managing Complex Change*. (2nd ed.) Boston: Addison-Wesley, 1987.

Boyatzis, R., McKee, A., and Goleman, D. "Reawakening Your Passion for Work." *Harvard Business Review*, 2002, 80(4), 86–94.

Cavafy, C. P. *The Complete Poems*. Athens, Greece: Ikarus, 1933.

Center for Creative Leadership. *Benchmarks Facilitators Manual*. Greensboro, N.C.: Center for Creative Leadership, 2000.

Chang, R. *The Passion Plan at Work*. San Francisco: Jossey Bass, 2001.

Cohen, S., and Bailey, D. "What Makes Teams Work: Group Effectiveness Research from the Shop Floor to the Executive Suite." *Journal of Management*, 1997, 23(3), 239–290.

Cooperrider, D., and Whitney, D. "A Positive Revolution in Change: Appreciative Inquiry." In D. Cooperrider and others (eds.), *Appreciative Inquiry: Rethinking Human Organization Toward a Positive Theory of Change*. Champaign, Ill.: Stiples, 2000.

Covey, S. R. *The Seven Habits of Effective People*. New York: Simon & Schuster, 1989.

Csiksentmihalyi, M. *Flow: The Psychology of Optimal Experience*. New York: HarperCollins, 1990.

Deming, W. E. *Out of the Crisis*. Cambridge, Mass.: MIT Press, 1986.

Doyle, M., and Straus, D. *How to Make Meetings Work*. New York: Jove Books, 1982.

Elbow, P. *Writing Without Teachers*. New York: Oxford University Press, 1973.

Hill, N. *Think and Grow Rich*. New York: Ballantine Books, 1996. (Originally published 1937)

Homer. *Odyssey* (trans. B. Fitzgerald). New York: Doubleday, 1961.

Jeffers, S. *Feel the Fear and Do It Anyway*. New York: Fawcett, 1987.

Jung, C. *Psychological Types*. Princeton, N.J.: Princeton University Press, 1971.

Kelley, T. *The Art of Innovation*. New York: Currency Doubleday, 2001.

Lewin, K. *Field Theory in Social Science*. New York: HarperCollins, 1951.

Livingston, J. "Pygmalion in Management." *Harvard Business Review*, 1969, 47(4), 81–89.

Myers, L. *Gifts Differing*. Palo Alto, Calif.: Consulting Psychologists Press, 1980.

Nadler, G., and Hibino, S. *Breakthrough Thinking: Why We Must Change the Way We Solve Problems and the Seven Principles to Achieve This*. Rocklin, Calif.: Prima, 1990.

Roos, J., and Victor, B. "Playing with Strategy." Paper presented at the 17th colloquium of the European Group for Organizational Studies, Lyon, France, July 5–7, 2001.

Senge, P. *The Fifth Discipline: The Art and Practice of the Learning Organization*. New York: Currency Doubleday, 1990.

Sutton, R. *Weird Ideas That Work: 11½ Practices for Promoting, Managing, and Sustaining Innovation*. New York: Free Press, 2002.

Talbot, M. "The Placebo Prescription." *New York Times Magazine*, January 9, 2000, p. 34.

Van de Ven, A. In *People and Technology in the Workplace*. Washington, D.C.: National Academy Press, 1991, p. 7.

"Voices: Inspiring Innovation." *Harvard Business Review*, 2002, 80(8), 39–49.

Von Oech, R. *Expect the Unexpected (or You Won't Find It): A Creativity Tool Based on the Ancient Wisdom of Heraclitus*. New York: Free Press, 2001.

Index

A

Absenteeism, 22
Abundance mentality, 6, 33–34
Acting As If exercise, 33
Action: fear and resistance to, 157–159; readiness for, 157–160; Solution Path step of, 5, 10, 11, 157–183; taking, 157–183
Action plan and planning, 5, 10, 157–183; books about, 189; case example of, 166–170, 174–175; for communicating the solution, 158, 171–174; designing, 160–171; dimensions of, 161–163; for evaluating the solution, 177–179; exercises for, 162–163, 165–166, 170–171, 173–174, 176, 178–179, 180–181; facilitation of, 163–164; key points about, 183; long-range, 161, 164, 165; participants in, 163–164; for planning future improvements, 179–181; readiness for action and, 157–160; risk minimization in, 161, 167, 170–171; short-range, 161, 164, 165–166; steps of, 161; for transition management, 174–176; worksheets for, 164–166
Active listening. See Listening, active
Advisory committee, transition management, 174–175
Aerospace industry case example, 15–17
Affirmations, 34–35; examples of, 34; exercise for, 35; for project, 123–124
Agenda: sample, 70–71; setting, 67–68
Airline industry, meal service redesign of, 153

Alternatives, 128–141; adding details to, 139–141; cost-benefit analysis of, 147–149; creating, 128–141; cross-fertilization of, 138–141, 146–147; deciding on, 142–152; discussing strengths and weaknesses of, 146; evaluating the benefits of, 143–144, 146; grouping ideas into, 132–138; ideas versus, 128–130; lobbying for, 147; merging or combining of, 139–141, 146–147; methods for working with, 138–141; overview of, 128–130; prioritizing ideas for, 106, 130–132, 134, 135; ranking, 149–151; review of, 152–153; working with, 138–141
Analysis: intuition versus, 143; starting with possibilities versus, 2
Apple Computer, 19, 82–83
Aristotle, 181
Asking questions. See Questions
Association technique, 111–112; dream analysis, 117; free, 112–114; metaphor and, 114

B

Bank work redesign case example, 61–62
Barriers: to action, 20–28, 157–159; fear as, 20–28, 140–142, 157–159
Beckhard, R., 174
Behavioral sciences, 1–2
Believing Game, 17–18, 128. See also Positive thinking
Bell, A. G., 61
Berlioz, H., 117
Blaming, 23–24; others, 23–24; in problem-focused approach, 81; self, 24